From Hurt to Happiness

Emotional Rescue

From the Ground Up

By

Mike Van

Text Copyright © 2013 Mike Van

All Rights Reserved

Driven 4 Success® (Australia)

Published by the Driven 4 Success Group

ISBN: 978-0-9875647-1-9

The moral right of the author has been asserted.

Without limiting the rights under copyright reserved above, no part of this publication may be reproduced, stored in or introduced into a retrieval system, or transmitted, in any form or by any means (electronic, mechanical, photocopying, recording or otherwise), without the prior written permission of both the copyright owner and the above publisher of this book.

Mike.van@fromhurttohappiness.com

www.fromhurttohappiness.com

Dedication

To my parents...

Had they not taken a gamble,

I might not be here today.

Contents

Dedication	3
Contents	4
Introduction	6
Lies That Destroy Relationships	23
All Too Typical Arguments	32
Truths No One Tells Us	40
Let Them Guide You	48
We Seek What Affirms Us	55
The Price Tag of the Need to be Right	61
The Cornerstone of Relationships	67
What We All Seek	82
Freedom to Breathe	91
In Search of Security	100
Love is a Choice, Not an Obligation	113
Not Always What They Want	120
Struggling to Share	127
It's Quality over Quantity of Time	136
Tokens to Remember	141
Yearning for a Connection	146
Love is the Art of Showing Affection	150
Vulnerability is a Choice	157
Apologizing Isn't Weakness	163

From Listening To Understanding	171
How We Misunderstand	179
Forgive but Don't Forget	183
Feel Their Pain	190
Nurture Loved Ones' Growth	196
They Hunger for Our Enthusiasm	205
Words from a Friend	209
APPENDIX	212
Love Association Exercise	212
Acknowledgments	216
Seeking More Answers	219

Introduction

Have you ever felt alone?

I mean *really* alone?

We have all had these moments - times when we feel alone, even when we're in a crowded room. We all have personal struggles we attempt to overcome. Try as we may, no one seems to truly understand our pain even though we try our best to explain and share it. At times, explaining how we feel is just not enough. Sadly, the only way for others to completely understand, would be for them to have experienced similar hardships. If this sounds familiar to you, know that you're not alone.

Throughout this book, I will share with you the many challenges I faced growing up, as well as what helped me to ultimately survive and overcome them. I will also explain how, through my experiences, I learned to connect with others and came to know the many secrets about relationships. My hope is that through my sharing, you will begin to find the answers to help you overcome your own struggles in life.

The idea for this book came to me during my second year of college. I was heading toward the tallest building on my university's campus with a suicide note clenched tightly in my hand. In hindsight, I can't pinpoint why I contemplated suicide or why I felt life was pointless and lacking. I honestly don't know. All I knew for sure was that I wanted *out*.

I suppose my spiral into such a desperate place began with my family. Our main family unit consists of first generation immigrants, which is a nicer way of saying that my family escaped a war-torn country with little more than the clothing on our backs.

When my parents left Vietnam, I was only several months old. We were struggling to evade imminent starvation and other deprivation. My father built makeshift rafts and sent many family members ahead in hopes of claiming a better future. This was during the monsoon season, so some unfortunates were swallowed up by the towering waves.

There were just two choices that could be made during those days; one was to take a gamble and risk death in order to give your young family a decent chance at a better future. Another was to stay put and slowly starve with scant hope of ever escaping poverty. My mother had just found out she was pregnant, so we took the gamble. We were fortunate enough to survive the treacherous waters and ward off starvation, only to find ourselves in a Malaysian refugee camp in 1986. It was here that my mother gave birth to my younger sister. My parents named her Viet-Dong to commemorate our struggle

- "Viet" for our country of origin and "Dong" to reflect our arrival in Malaysia.[1]

These were our humble beginnings in a new land. While I was too young to remember the details myself, I have been told that it felt more like a jail than a camp, but my still family endured. Four years after our initial escape from Vietnam, in 1989, we were allowed to immigrate to Australia, which was the beginning of our journey as Australian citizens.

During these early years, there was a swarm of Vietnamese refugees seeking shelter. The Australian government didn't quite know how to handle the multiplying numbers of all those arriving on their shores. My parents didn't speak English and possessed very few skills, other than working in the rice paddy fields, which only made our plight even harder. Everyone was trying to adjust. Some families handled the transition better than others. However, those who held on to their pasts tended to fare worse. My family belonged to this latter category.

I have no conscious memories of these events. I learned of them through the stories my parents and relatives told me over the years. The earliest memory I have is of my family being relocated to a new home when the government decided where we would be sent. So there we were, in a strange new land, immersed in a cornucopia of different cultures, and trying to create a new life from scratch.

---

[1] Viet from Vietnam while Dong from "Bi Dong" the Vietnamese traditional word for Malaysia.

I attended a public school and dreaded every single day of it. I was able to get the education my parents lacked, and; therefore desired for their children. For many people, school can be a place of joy. For me, it was a nightmare. We were among the first Asian families in the community and I was a late developer (I did not utter my first word until I was five). I soon became the easy and convenient emotional punching bag for school bullies. Our suburb was considered by outsiders to be "government housing" and crime infested. It wasn't like that, though, because the families who lived there were simply struggling to get by. Looking back, I realize now that the bullies were also struggling with their own frustrations. They were hurting, and felt the need to take it out on someone else - I just happened to be a suitable scapegoat.

My family carried a bundle of emotional baggage. My father was quick-tempered; although, in his defense, much of it was the by-product of his time spent at war. He was conscripted into service, and the only way to get out was to spend time in a jail cell, where the chances of survival were slimmer than they were on the battlefields. When he returned from the frontlines, the only type of work he could find was hard labor. He didn't have much choice in the matter. Back then, if you wanted to put food on the table, you took whatever job was available. Food was scarce, but men were plentiful. Looking at the scars on my father's right forearm and left calf from bullet wounds, I simply cannot fathom the torment he must have gone through. He was forced to leave school at the tender age of ten to work on a farm because if you didn't work, you didn't eat. Growing up, the only things that kept him going were fear, anger, hurt, and violence. He became the perfect soldier. Weakness and compassion would only get him killed.

During much of my youth, I resented my father's anger as he took out most of his frustration, both physical and emotional, on us, his family. Memories of his anger still linger on clearly with me. There were times when I woke up to my family having just survived another one of my father's bouts of rage and depression. One such time, my parents had one of their all too common arguments. When my father returned home later in the day, angry and in a drunken stupor, he poured gasoline around the outside of the house with the intention of burning my mother and us four children in our sleep. Another incident happened on Christmas Day, when my mother was able to escape from his vicious clutches and hid us in a support group home for beaten women. My father went around physically threatening my aunties (my mother's sisters) until we came back home. Knowing his history and knowing his temperament, his threats were never to be taken lightly.

As much as it hurts and angers me to recollect such painful memories, when I look at my father, and know more stories about his life, I can't help but see him in a new light. Life was tough, not only on us, his family, but for him also.

One particular incident happened when I was twenty-five years old, as I was helping him with some work he was doing. My father received a call from his older sister back home in Vietnam. She was so distraught that I could literally hear her sobs on the other end of the line. She had called to let him know their younger brother had just died from liver cancer. After the short exchange, he hung up.

I looked into his eyes to search for signs of sadness, only for him to stare back at me and respond with, "That's life." He went right back to work as if nothing had happened. I moved toward him to hug him, but as I wrapped my arms around his body, he just stood there motionless. Even though he didn't say a word, I could feel his heavy breathing and a slight trembling in his arms. I could sense he desperately wanted to hug me back. The tears threatened in his eyes; however, he refused to let them fall. In that moment, I realized the reason behind his attitude was not that he didn't care about us, or didn't feel affection; it was that he didn't know *how* to let go and express his sorrow. He had spent his entire life being strong, so he wasn't able to open up and show his true self to others.

In that moment, I felt the need to tell him I loved him - words I had never uttered to him in the twenty-five years I'd been his son. I hadn't said it until then either because I believed he didn't need to know it, or because I wasn't sure if I did. My feelings toward him until that point had always been jumbled up and mixed. I had hated and loved him all at the same time.

Watching him then, I came to realize just how many of people struggle with showing affection and compassion. My father loved us in his own way even though it was just difficult for him to show it in a manner that we could fully understand and appreciate. Many of us tend to believe our fathers do not require love because they are the strong ones. This idea is a lie. We spend our time telling our mothers how much we love them, but never utter the same words to our fathers, because society tells us that this is "normal."

It took me a long time to realize my father was never *trying* to hurt us. He was just struggling with his own fears and dark past. His words may never have been elegant, but he was always there when we needed him. He showed us love through his actions and the little things he did for us. Many of us are too focused on our own pain and fears to notice the simple gestures others make that enrich our lives. So much love is unspoken.

My mother has her own story. She was the product of a society that taught women to believe they deserved very little from life and from other people. Back then, women were taught to obey their husbands. Their solitary role was to serve men, deliver and raise children, and tolerate being misused and abused. She was punished routinely for "crimes" she never even committed. The eldest girl of eight children, my mother lost her parents when she was in her early twenties. She was thrown into responsibilities she wasn't prepared for at the time. She had her own fears and worries, and suffered from bouts of depression well into adulthood. Untold, bottled up inside, her story passed silently, insidiously down to her young family. As loving as she tried to be, she couldn't help but react to her fears and hurts, lashing out at those she loved most.

Life was hard. My parents were often emotionally absent even when they were physically present. They were often lost in their own memories and upbringings; they were busy fighting their own fears and insecurities.

Because recent immigrants like my parents lacked English and mainstream job skills, they had to accept whatever work was offered just to get by. They were so unsure as to who to trust that they became easy prey for business people with questionable moral compasses. Sadly, many immigrants end up being exploited. Like my mother - I remember coming home from school, after a day of being bullied and tormented, to help my mother in the little sweatshop we had in our house. She sat at a sewing machine from six in the morning to ten at night every day, taking breaks only to cook meals. Despite the long hours, she was paid a measly few dollars for all of her efforts. No matter how hard my parents and others like them worked, they were denied even minimum wage. They knew so little about their rights; they just accepted what was offered.

Sometimes my mother would rummage through the city trash bins for half-eaten stale chips or to collect waste lettuce leaves that supermarkets threw out to take home so we would have something to eat. Schools in Australia weren't like the schools in the United States. It wasn't the responsibility of the government to make sure students had something to eat for lunch. Many times I went to school with an empty stomach. I learned to make some extra money by buying noodle packets in bulk and selling them individually at school for a profit, just so I could afford something for lunch.

This was the typical lifestyle for most third world immigrants in Australia. Few of us had access to education in our home countries so we had to do with what we knew. Vietnam, at the time of our departure, was still devastated by war and lack of food. Landmines and deadly traps, remnants from combat, still littered Vietnam's landscape. Food was so scarce that starvation was a common theme. More than half of the population was unemployed.[2]

War has the tendency to bring out the ugliness of human nature, not just during, but also in the aftermath of it all. Those in power oppressed and took advantage of those worse off. Frequently, the ones who were doing the oppressing were the police and the local government. The country was still trying to find its feet, and this was even more evident where we came from, the far off rural parts of Vietnam.

When you come from a world where corruption is the norm, it's hard to know who you can trust. Most of the time, you couldn't rely on anyone. For us, distrust spread because we felt everyone we knew was trying to take advantage of us. The people who were supposed to protect us were the ones we were wary of the most. We continued to associate the "government" and "police" with the corrupt officials we remembered back home in Vietnam.

Growing up in Australia, my siblings and I were forced to constantly move from one

---

2 http://lcweb2.loc.gov/frd/cs/profiles/Vietnam.pdf

community to another. In the beginning we were always changing schools. Fortunately, we found our way into a little Vietnamese community where everyone had been displaced as well. Everyone within the neighborhood understood how it felt to be lost in a foreign country with little understanding of the language or marketable skills to fall back on.

Upon enrolling in my new school, I was overjoyed. The majority of the students were also fellow Vietnamese immigrants. I was relieved because I was finally able to escape the bullying that tormented me since childhood. By then I was fifteen years old and had been bullied for more than ten of those years. The constant teasing and picking on left me socially awkward, fearful, and defensive. I always assumed others were just out to get me in some way. This wasn't paranoia; it was a reflection of what was once my daily reality.

All I knew of the world up to this point was fear and hurt. The day I changed schools, I adopted a new name – Mike - to symbolize my aspiration to gain freedom and peace. I started to make a conscious effort to learn how to connect with others. It was a struggle of monumental proportions. Learning even the simplest, most basic social skills was tough because I was constantly fighting the urge to listen to the old messages that ran non-stop in my head: violence, defensiveness, pain, fear, anger, and depression.

Starting from scratch, I learned to smile and laugh freely, something most people take for granted. During this time, I questioned many of the assumptions I held about myself, others, and the world, presuming what I had known and understood up to that point was incomplete helped me tremendously. This mindset kept my mind open to new information and insight, a habit that continues to serve me well to this day.

Initially, my progress was slow. At times it seemed to be non-existent. But through my struggle, I came to realize that many others were also dealing with challenges. My plight and fears weren't unique; they were different only because they were personal to me. I had to learn so many things that may have seemed obvious to most people. Everyone has a starting point and carries their own personal baggage of some sort, and so we just have to make do with what we have and move on from there.

My starting point began when I changed schools. It was godsend. Although I had fear bubbling inside of me, I climbed out of my emotional limb to make my first real connection with first real friend, Khang. At the time, Khang was the only person who made me feel as if I belonged, which was a major milestone for me! Trusting another person wasn't easy if your belief system has already been established that, "sooner or later everyone will disappoint you."

Over the next couple of years, I became much more comfortable around others. Unfortunately, some of the people I befriended weren't the greatest of influences. Due to our surroundings and circumstances, my friendships were determined more by proximity than by shared interests. At times, I befriended people out of what felt like necessity.

During these years, the Vietnamese community continued to grow. Refugees flocked to the area and small businesses (restaurants and Asian groceries) started popping up all over the place. The Australian government carried out a social experiment by letting local people form their own communities with little outside governance.

By the time my family relocated to one of these communities it was already in semi-recovery. However, the area still had a crime rate far higher than the neighborhood we had left. There were gangs and rivalries among various groups. Our suburb was well known for its drug dealers. The local Vietnamese gangs thrived by exploiting their own people. It wasn't safe to walk the streets at night. Junkies overdosed on park benches and in alleyways. Our community was the first and only place in Australia where a local politician was assassinated. In a nutshell, it was a cesspool of drugs and violence.

In retrospect, what happened seems preordained by circumstances. Letting a displaced community with a strong distrust of the government and police attempt to resolve a major drug problem while at the same time trying to find its way in the world was a disaster in the making. Thankfully, things have greatly improved since those times. The streets became cleaner and fear no longer lingers around every corner. Many of the younger locals are now second and third generation Viet-Aussies, complete with the accent. When the government finally intervened, the community began to flourish. It took time, but many of those who were displaced eventually adjusted to their new home and refers to themselves "Australians." Nevertheless, behind this pleasant veneer lays a very dark history. Although the violence and drug culture has since subsided, their effects linger on in a community where there are still enough people who remember the "bad old" days.

Much of my transformation took place while I was in high school. Unfortunately, many of my friends and their families still struggled to adjust to a new culture and lifestyle. Most of the guys I befriended dropped out of school to chase the allure of easy money via drugs and violence, or they were being forced to help their families find ways to make ends meet. It was also during this time that I started to take my studies more seriously. I had never paid much attention in school until I arrived there, nor had I been able to get away from the constant threat of bullies. Even though it was hard, I didn't fall into the same "drugs and violence" trap that claimed so many of my friends. Some of them ended up in jail, while others faired much worse. Had I stayed on the same path, my future would have looked equally bleak. After my friends left, my grades greatly improved.

One night, while preparing for exams and assignments, my phone rang. On the other end was a frantic voice, sobbing, "Khang just died!" I sat there shell-shocked. Khang had been shot by a party crasher the night before. The bullet pierced his face and, as he collapsed, the shooter ran forward to stomp on Khang's head to make sure he was dead. From that point on, numbness overcame me. I focused solely on finding ways to get out of the area, to get away from the friends I once knew, trading one hurt for a new one.

The tough outer shell I built for myself seemed to be working when it led me to the university. However, with the constant arguments at home, I was continually frustrated trying to get my studies under control. My resolve began to chip away bit by bit. Cracks started to show and the horrid thought of finding peace at last by ending it all began to flicker through my mind. The next thing I knew, I found myself walking toward the tallest building on campus with a suicide note clutched in my hand.

Looking back on that day, as bleak and depressing as it may have been, I can't help but be eternally grateful for having been so close to the edge. I still cannot explain what went through my mind that day or during the weeks before. Whatever it was, the toll was making itself known as I neared my limits. But, pulling myself away from the brink of despair and fighting back the lingering depression that had plagued me since childhood, I came to realize I could never feel worse than I did that day. For me, that one day was yet another turning point - another of many "wake up" calls I would have in my life.

The pervasive pain led me to scour through books and spend years searching my soul, trying to uncover answers to some of life's toughest questions, such as: Why do we hurt ourselves and each other? Why do some relationships blossom while others struggle? It also spurred years of coming to terms with this question that plagued me:

Am I deserving of continued happiness? The only happiness I had known up to that point was fleeting and it had always been replaced by hurt.

It may seem strange that someone would question whether or not they were deserving of happiness, but that was exactly how it was for me. I always doubted whether I was worthy of love, always questioned if I was lovable. Trying to come to terms with my self-worth was especially difficult when all I had seen around me were dysfunctional relationships: my own, those of my relatives, friends, siblings, parents — people who supposedly loved each other, yet continued to hurt everyone else in their orbit.

Although the circumstances I found myself in as a child weren't ideal for my development, they served as a major motivation to understand the dynamics of human relationships. By watching and listening, I learned what not to do. I began to understand how and why we hurt each other. Very soon, all the pieces came together and the connections began to reveal themselves. I comprehended that much of learning was actually a process of *unlearning*. Realizing how old, destructive habits caused our current pain and overcoming those behaviors can free us to see new possibilities. Learning to see circumstances and people through another person's perspective and not our own feelings and emotions was transformative.

It was difficult to learn how to openly accept others when one was accustomed to being a social outcast. Learning how to show love and affection was especially difficult when it felt like it was never shown to you. My paradigm was, "We all teach what we know; if all we know is hurt, it will be the only thing we're capable of teaching." Through my own struggle, I came to realize that it doesn't have to be that way at all. Observing my past objectively for the first time in my life taught me that although our past shapes us into who we are today, it doesn't have to define who we will be tomorrow, next week, or next year. At first, the changes we make toward a better tomorrow and becoming a better person may seem slow, while other times, these changes may seem impossible. That being said, when we start from where we are and watch what happens tomorrow, next week, and next year, we find ourselves amazed, surprised, and delighted with the changes that will ultimately be revealed.

It was a challenging journey, but worth the time and effort. With practice, many new skills became second nature. We don't always get it right at first, but persistence will surely lead us to better places where we can enjoy healthier relationships with those who are most precious to us.

This isn't meant to be a sad story. On the contrary, I hope it will give you hope, courage, and most importantly - a plan. The fact that you're reading this means you also believe there's a better option out there than constant hurting. Picking up this book is a major step toward improving your life and relationships.

Meeting me now, you would never imagine my past. Just like what happened to me, happiness is very much within your grasp. Even though I haven't walked in your shoes, I hope you will benefit from the lessons I have learned while walking down my own path to transformation and joy.

"Happiness is not given,

it is earned."

Chapter 1

Lies That Destroy Relationships

Every relationship has its highs and lows. Every relationship is both a blessing and a curse. When it's good, it's great. We feel a sense of belonging, so much that we want to become better people because we feel nurtured and supported. We want to return the blessing.

When it's bad, it's awful. We feel we're emotionally under siege and become defensive and fearful. Unsure of the other person's intentions, we can experience paranoia and lash out in anger.

Looking back on my dark years, I simply didn't understand what makes us lash out at the people we love the most. Even though we would never truly want to hurt them, at times our emotions break loose and we can't help but take it out on them. I hated how I would react whenever I became hurt or upset – unable to share, always easily irritated, frustrated, feeling that others are trying to hurt me. No matter their niceness, the kindness others might have shown, I always had a lingering doubt as to if their friendly were genuine or if there were hidden agendas behind it. I just assumed the worst about people and at the slightest inkling of confrontation, my defensiveness went up – I had an oversensitive trigger that made me prone to being

aggressive and confrontational with people.
Looking back at the situations in hindsight, at times its because of seemingly trivial matters. I wanted to understand what was going on inside my head that caused me react like so. This mystery afflicted me for years until I finally began looking for answers.

Finding others in struggling relationships was easy. All I had to do was look around me. There were plenty of people. Listening to the comments of friends and family, and watching how trivial matters could escalate into full-blown arguments with both parties yelling, offered plenty of clues. By paying careful attention, I began to notice common themes.

It was clear that both sides cared about each other. We would never form or remain in a relationship with another person if we didn't care about them. Yet, time and time again, whenever hurt flares, arguments escalate. As this happens, many of us tend to go on autopilot, blaming and criticizing the other. Many of us are unable to control ourselves even though we know we're being hurtful. It's as though we just can't seem to stop ourselves.

After decades of frustration and hurting, I eventually came to realize there were questions hidden underneath why I felt this way or reacted in a hurtful manner toward another person: "Do you care for me? If so, why are you hurting me?" I wondered if others faced the same questions. When I began to finally listen not to what others *said*, but how they *felt,* I was able to see things in a new light.

It seems that during any relationship conflict

many of us have very similar underlying doubts. We often feel unsure about ourselves and worry that our loved ones might *not* love or care about us. We are so busy feeling hurt we don't realize we're actually wounding the ones we love. We become more focused on our own hurt without considering others. It should be the other way around. We let our frustration reach a point where both parties feel drained and resentful. Why do we do this, and let our arguments escalate so much that neither party feels loved or cared for?

Watching these exchanges between two people, I noticed one or both of them tend to withdraw. They hide behind an emotional wall whenever they felt attacked, blamed, or criticized, until they spot an opening to lash out — and wounding the other. Lips that were previously springs of tenderness became weapons, discharging sharp, bitter retorts and snide remarks. At times things got so bad that both parties ended up seething with a resentment that never healed until a break-up or divorce inevitably followed.

In listening to stories about why so many relationships fail, something struck me. When asked why their relationships failed, many people offered the same set of reasons. The claim their relationship ended because it was their partner's fault. These answers never completely satisfied me.

I felt there had to be a simpler, more straightforward reason, something so obvious that many were oblivious to it. Relationships do not just fail. There is always a cause, because relationships start out precious and compelling. Even though we may not see or understand it, there is always a reason, sometimes more than one reason.

Piecing the puzzle together, I began to notice the dynamics that end relationships. Whenever we're hurting, what we say or do to others can come out haphazardly. Even though we're trying to show affection, our words are often inadequate. When we feel criticized, we automatically become defensive. We develop a severe lack of trust and tolerance for each other's shortcomings. In the relationships I've observed, there is a constant animosity that begins to linger, one that makes both parties fearful of being hurt. No one wants to share because they fear they might be misunderstood and hurt if they give too much of themselves. This is the same fear that makes us doubt our loved ones' commitment and makes us deny we may be at fault. We scoff at the idea that we may be the ones struggling to show affection and that what we're showing may come across as being insensitive. We ridicule others because we're afraid to admit we simply don't know how to love another person in the way he or she wishes to be loved.

Often, we are quick to blame the other person for our hurt, even though it may not originate from what our loved ones did or didn't do for us, but instead from what we needed but were unable to get from them. In our desire to be a part of a healthy and fulfilling relationship, we often feel it is our loved ones' duty to make the relationship work, it is their responsibility to make us happy, creating the safe haven where we feel loved and secure so we can share ourselves openly and honestly. We fool ourselves, and our friends can reinforce this flawed belief, that the fault always lies with our partners or ex-partners. We refuse to accept that each person plays the part of both victim *and* culprit in *every* relationship.

Have you ever noticed that the things we dislike most in others are usually the things we dislike most about ourselves? It's easier to be on the offensive than to justify and defend ourselves against criticism. We complain that people don't listen; however, do we truly listen when they share their thoughts and feelings? Who is pushing who away? Our fear of being hurt is so great that we rarely let ourselves become vulnerable to others. This is how things become so bad that we end up attacking each other.

There is also the need to test each other. Where do we get this need to test those we love - to test their commitment and their willingness to stand by us? We continue to test others even though we know that by testing them, it may very well cost us the relationship we so desperately want to preserve and protect.

On a day-to-day basis, it's difficult enough to understand what to give, what to say, or what to do to ease a loved one's stress and frustration, though many of us make it even harder than it needs to be. By acting solely on our own emotions, we fail to realize our loved ones are acting merely upon their emotions as well. To avoid being hurt, we cultivate assumptions along the way without questioning them. Assumptions can cause grief because, in our attempt to avoid getting hurt, we may actually create even more misery. We don't stop the hurt or fear with our assumptions. All we do is trade one anxiety for another and we fail to realize that in a relationship each partner faces his or her own set of problems and challenges. In an attempt to protect ourselves, we build a wall that inevitably pushes away those we love.

By really listening, we slowly begin to recognize the assumptions others hold about themselves and the people around them, as well as expectations they live by daily and never consider questioning. When I listened to others and realized how much grief their assumptions were causing them, I started wondering about my own. What was it I unwittingly believed about the world? How did my expectations lead me to my past predicaments? And, if I didn't confront them, how would they lead to future undesired predicaments?

Many of our assumptions are developed and nurtured when we are at our lowest points in life, when we are weak and hurting. In an attempt to protect ourselves, we subconsciously draw conclusions and build suppositions. My traumatic experiences left me emotionally scarred, hurting, and worried, and I made a silent promise to myself that I would never experience such hurt again. In trying to live up to that vow, I mentally agreed never to make myself vulnerable to anyone else. Many people have made similar promises to themselves (consciously or subconsciously); the only difference is in how they live up to fulfill them.

Your own assumptions can be complex or simple. I found that I was living by many of them. As I grew older and learned more about myself and others, I had to unravel them to see how each was a lie, and posed a threat to my happiness and well-being:

- My partner should understand me well enough to know what to do and say.
- When others hurt me, it is intentional.
- Whenever I'm hurting, someone or something else is responsible.
- My partner doesn't understand me because he or she doesn't care enough.
- Relationships should be effortless.
- Love is a game; all is fair and I can take what I need.
- My partner should accommodate me before I accommodate them.
- If my partner isn't willing to give to me, why should I give to them?
- My partner has no right to hurt me, or say anything that hurts me.
- Treat them mean to keep them keen.
- Always have the upper hand.
- If my partner is ever deemed to be right, that means I am deemed to be wrong.
- Relationships are complicated and will only lead to hurt.

When we believe assumptions such as these, we're playing a back and forth game of emotional tag—waiting, dodging, and trying to get our wants and needs met before considering the other person's requirements. As I constantly waited for the safe time to give or share myself, it became more difficult. When I finally did decide to share, my guard was up, expecting at any moment to be hurt or criticized by others. At the slightest sign of resistance or confrontation, I assumed the worst. I waited for someone to be receptive to my needs and then waited for them to notice my hurt. I wasted so much of my life always waiting for the "safe moment" but the time never came. No matter how much I tried to avoid it, the possibility of getting hurt was ever-present.

The fear of being hurt, which is behind these assumptions, can all too often lead us to adopt an "us versus them" attitude toward our loved ones. We become suspicious of each other, looking for reasons to be disappointed, competing over which one of us is hurting more and relentlessly trying to prove who's right and who's wrong in the relationship. We even compete to prove who's more lovable or worthy. Relationships simply cannot prosper this way. In fact, given the way so many of us cripple them from day one because the emotional baggage we drag along, they can be doomed from the onset.

Do you have any of these assumptions? They can be deadly traps waiting unwittingly to trip us, causing unnecessary frustrations in our relationships. Take some time out to think about which of these assumptions you may have unknowingly adopted, and why.

"First and foremost, question your assumptions about yourself, others and the world; they are often not true."

Chapter 2

All Too Typical Arguments

As much as we strive to avoid hurting one another, it is simply not always possible. Hurt is part and parcel of every relationship, as emotions are ever present. Since we can't be in control of anyone else's emotions, we'll always be subject to the fear of being hurt by them. This fear is unavoidable, so hurting each other is always possible. Perhaps overcoming the hurt can be achieved by the act of embracing the fear and acknowledging up front the very real possibility of getting hurt. As the saying goes, we should, "feel the fear and do it anyway," because hurting each other is so rarely intentional. Caring for one another, while trying to protect ourselves, can so frequently come across as an attack.

There are many ways to avoid being hurt, but when we choose to flee out of fear of being hurt, we allow our fear to dictate our fate. Many of us have our guards up and are defensive even *before* our partner begins to share their feelings. We remain guarded because we anticipate blame or an attack, even when all they're simply sharing is the desire to communicate their frustrations or concerns with us. At times, what seems to be an accusation, in fact is a plea for us to care, to show them that they matter to us.

Wounded psyches are all too often unable to see that their partner's troubles are not a reflection of themselves. We constantly relate issues back to ourselves and our own (real or imagined) culpability, so when we feel attacked, we retaliate. We are so busy trying to justifying our view; so adamant about making our thoughts and feelings heard first, that we often can't see or realize we're actually making our loved ones feel worse about themselves. Rather than letting them express themselves freely without the fear of being criticized, we add an unspoken clause: "I will only listen if I don't feel like I am being attacked." But it's hard to embrace their hurt when we may actually be the cause of that hurt, not because we're at fault or because they blame us, but because they have grown to love us and we are so sensitive to their words and actions. The more we become attached to another person, the more vulnerable and susceptible we become to feeling hurt and rejected by the person we have come to love.

As they become more important to us, we begin to develop greater expectations from them. We listen, already assuming the worst, until eventually we end up hurting both ourselves and our loved ones. As our level of hurt escalates, we can become unresponsive to other person's troubles. We're too busy trying to be the first to get our own point across that we don't bother listening or even acknowledging the other person's feelings. When we finally slow down long enough to take a step back and review the situation, we notice that our partner is every bit as fearful and hurt as we are, and worried that we may no longer love or care for them.

When we feel our partners aren't willing to listen to us, we can often berate them, because it feels like they're unwilling to consider our welfare unless we put a spotlight on it. Most of us, at one time or another, have known what it feels like to be on the receiving end of a partner's wrath and scorn. When we're feeling coerced, we can choose to cave in to the pressure and simply complying with their wishes. To keep the peace and avoid escalating the argument, we oblige. It's easier to avoid the tongue-lashing than to justify why we feel compromised or coerced. But when we do this, we're easily left feeling bitter and resentful.

Sometimes when we feel pressured and forced, we instead choose to fight back. Perhaps it's because we don't want to feel controlled and we want to feel as though we are preserving our freedom. If we agree to their demands, it will cost our right to choose in the future. What we may have previously agreed to do willingly could now feel as though we're being pushed into it, so we get angry, become defiant, and fight back. All too often, we're simply fighting ourselves. And either way, whether we cave or fight back, we end up feeling hurt and frustrated.

What *is* this defiant nature within that stirs us to fight, argue, and hurt those we know who would never intentionally try to hurt us? One likely answer is that our defiance is fed by our doubts and fears. Every time I have allowed others to share with me and I refrained from reacting negatively or interrupting them, they became more willing and receptive to my own concerns. Much of the frustration that builds within relationships is really the result of fears and doubts being triggered. When we insist on interrupting, correcting, and defending ourselves, it only makes our loved ones feel criticized (triggering their fear that we are attacking or rejecting them), or it can give them the impression that their feelings aren't important or justified. In trying to substantiate our own feelings, we can end up belittling theirs. There's a fine line between sharing our concerns and belittling others - a fine line many of us cross unwittingly.

    Many times in the past when I have tried to share myself, I realized it wasn't just about me listening to others. It was also about the feeling of being heard and knowing I mattered to them. Whenever I became defensive and frustrated, it was actually my own fears being triggered—the fear that my partners weren't seeing me in the same light, or didn't care for me in the same way I cared for them. It was this fear that made me feel the need to force them to listen to me. It was this same fear that made me argue, because I figured that, if they really cared, they would see things the way I saw them. But because I was so busy trying to get my feelings heard, I didn't realize that they were also acting upon the same set of fears. It was only when I started to put a greater focus on making sure *they* felt heard and their concerns and worries mattered, that they became equally receptive to mine.

    Our partners' frustrations with us might not about whether we're listening or not. Just because we hear what they say doesn't mean our partners' perspectives will be embraced or honored as if we shared the same perspective. When our partners feel that they matter, their voices are heard, and they can express themselves freely without the fear that we might become defensive or critical of their opinions, we achieve full partnership and begin to trust each other.

When we become irritated, especially when it's over something related to a loved one, we try to express our frustration as a concern, hoping they'll notice it's not meant as an attack, but simply as subjective frustration and hurt. Unfortunately, instead of embracing our pain or hearing what we share as a plea, they can misinterpret what we are attempting to say as criticism. It isn't that we're trying to hurt our loved ones; all we really want is for them to notice how much they are hurting us. However, instead of perceiving it as us being "hurt," they feel as though we are blaming them. Rather than honoring our pain, they upset us even more by trying to defend themselves. The cycle of hurt and defense can continue to a point where both parties feel they are getting nowhere and neither party cares or is willing to listen. We end up blaming our partners for their defensiveness – but is it really their fault? Could it boil down to assumptions we have about them and love relationships that are rearing their ugly heads?

Whenever we feel criticized, it can be easy to become defensive. We defend ourselves from what appear to be attacks on our wounded egos. What would happen if we tried to set the wounded ego aside and express ourselves differently? What if we reassured our loved ones from the very beginning that what we're sharing is in no way a criticism or blame, and that it's actually a cry, a plea for them to notice that our fears are simply being triggered and we need to be assured that we're still the light and joy of their life? If we did this, don't you think others would be more receptive to what we are sharing with them? You bet they would!

While many of us interpret the frustrations of others as personal attacks, in reality this is rarely the case. I know how hard it is to share when feeling attacked, but the more we try to defend ourselves, the more our loved ones will be the ones to feel hurt. When I started to see my loved ones as emotional beings who, like me, struggled with their feelings, I realized just how much of their frustration may stem from inner hurts. So instead of defending myself, I started to shift my focus toward their worries and fears. The more I was able to ease their frustration and hurt, the less they felt the need to defend or retaliate. By shifting my focus, I began to notice the effect my words and actions has on them, instead of regarding them as being wrong and trying to justify my own actions. This simple shift in focus on the other person made all the difference. No longer giving in to the urge to defend myself helped change the way my partners perceived me. They no longer questioned my intentions because I no longer questioned theirs.

It was by truly witnessing and taking to heart my mother's teary eyes and my father's frustration-laden brows, and reading the careworn lines that were etched into both of their faces, that I came to see a lurking secret that so many of us miss out in today's fast-paced world – the need to be accepted. If we truthfully look into the eyes of the people we encounter, we'll see that yearning brewing inside of them. We're all struggling with the same challenge of finding someone who would accept and appreciate us. Even though we may have different ways of dealing with hurt and confrontation, much of our angst stems from the same place: the desire to freely express ourselves and find acceptance and reassurance. The only way in which we can accurately make it safe for ourselves to feel this, is by first making it safe for others to share. By offering our loved ones a safe place to share, we make it safe for us to do the same.

I chanced upon this insight by watching others argue. Rather than playing the blame game (deciding who is right or wrong), I placed myself on both sides, trying to discern the thoughts that might be running through each person's mind, while trying to understand the emotions swelling in the other. As I watched the sparring partners, I noticed the same thoughts and feelings repeated endlessly. Many of us deal with our frustrations in the same way. I know I have. In arguments, these are the actions I see all the time:

➢ Trying to defend or justify ourselves from accusations of having done something wrong.

➢ Complaining that others are ungrateful or unappreciative of our efforts.

➢ Bringing past faults into current arguments.

➢ Listing each other's shortcomings or failings.

➢ Competing with each other as to who feels most hurt.

➤ Getting so frustrated that we withdraw, frequently letting our loved ones deal with their frustrations alone.

➤ Refusing to reconcile; no matter how much we want to reach out, we don't. We're hurting so much that we can't bear the thought of another confrontation.

➤ Insulting each other with degrading names, or trying to inflict anguish on our loved ones to hurt them as much as they're hurting us.

These are only some of the patterns or traps we fall into that create and escalate all too typical arguments. The more aware we are, the sooner we are able to snap out of the pattern. To do this means realizing our fears, letting go of our defensiveness, and focusing on the other person first from a place of love.

"The things we dislike most about others are usually the things we struggle against most within ourselves."

Chapter 3

Truths No One Tells Us

No one wants to be part of a conflict that escalates to the point where we start to insult each other, tossing out hurtful, degrading names. But, when we're frustrated, we often feel justified in thrusting the responsibility for calming the situation into the hands of our sparring partners, forgetting that we, too, play a role in whatever reaction they're displaying toward us. We justify hurting them as being warranted. After all, they hurt us first, right? Not always. Even though we may feel injured, it does not imply that the fault lies elsewhere.

This revelation came to me from one particular event. I was sitting in a café enjoying the start of the day with a nice hot latte. Sitting to my right were a couple of women complaining and bickering about their partners. Their conversation piqued my interest. I heard a vicious outpouring about the many things their respective partners had done wrong during the course of their relationships. The more I listened, the more I realized that only insults and slurs were being offered. Not a single word of praise was uttered on behalf of their partners.

Nothing they said made sense to me, and I wanted clarification. I decided to interrupt to seek their feminine perspective on things. This seemed a prime opportunity to try and demystify "the war between the sexes."

I introduced myself to the two ladies I'll call Jane and Sarah. They both just got out of a two year relationship. Recognizing their bitterness and resentment toward their former partners, I couldn't help but wonder if I'd gotten myself into trouble. Had I just volunteered to be the scapegoat for their frustrations?

As we talked, it dawned on me that what they were expressing wasn't really anger, rather a sense of abandonment. Each woman felt unloved or unlovable, so the only way it seemed they could cope with the breakup was to cast themselves as the victim and make their partner the culprit.

They told me stories about their partners being emotionally distant and uncaring. One story in particular, about Sarah and her partner, Peter, was very instructive. Sarah had been left devastated when her parents divorced. In her pain, she turned to Peter seeking solace and comfort. Instead of receiving love, care, and affection, she found him cold and insensitive. She said all he did was mutter a few words about everything being all right and that she should relax. In a fit of frustration, she lashed out at him. This led to a downward spiral that eventually ended their relationship. Sarah labeled Peter as unaffectionate, emotionally retarded, and absent.

As Sarah and Jane shared their stories, something unsettling stirred inside me. It dawned on me that I had experienced similar situations in which I had been expected to comfort a partner. Many times in my earlier years, I stumbled with my words. I tried to be caring, but because I had been unsure of how my partner would react, I held back and stopped trying to explain myself. This seemed to have been the case with Peter. Apparently, he tried to be supportive, but Sarah didn't recognize his feeble attempts and got upset. Sarah had expected him to know all the right words to say and comfort her, not considering that he, too, had been worried about also being hurt. It wasn't that he didn't care; it was that he didn't know how to show it in a language of love she could understand. Because he was unsure if he could make her feel better, he held back.

    We all put our guard up and hold back from time to time, particularly when we feel threatened or insecure. If we can't predict what we share as being one hundred percent accepted by our partner, then more often than not, we choose to retreat. We choose to hold back and not risk it. In Peter's case, he felt that by sharing himself it would have made him more vulnerable to Sarah. Not understanding this, Sarah thought of him as insensitive when, in truth, he might have been as doubtful and worried as she was. Rather than share her fears and/or express her hurts, she attacked – calling Peter many hurtful names in an attempt at trying to force him to give in to her. Because he feared more attacks, because his efforts were going unnoticed, as feeble as they were, he withdrew and gave up trying to comfort her, feeling unappreciated and seething with resentment. Why should he try to comfort someone who didn't acknowledge his efforts? Sarah hadn't noticed he might have been struggling with being affectionate with her. Peter was unsure if she would see his attempts for what they were. He felt unsure whether he could make difference in her well-being, and if his words of encouragement would be welcomed no matter how poorly he expressed himself. Can anyone of us freely share who we are when we feel our partners may be constantly frustrated with us, their parents, themselves, others or the world?

In my conversation with these ladies, I tried to play devil's advocate to humanize their partners. However, that only exacerbated their frustration. To my mind, Peter wouldn't even have tried muttering words of concern in the first place had he not cared. But because Sarah had been frustrated, she hadn't noticed that he, too, had been fearful of being hurt. Whenever she had lashed out, she simply confirmed his fear: "If I open myself up try to comfort her, I will only get hurt, so why bother?"

As much as I wanted to tell them my opinions, it seems they wouldn't be receptive. Instead, it was as if they were relishing in their victim roles. Seeing things from their partners' perspectives would have forced them to relinquish their anger, and instead feel sad and guilty about the abandonment that they had helped orchestrate.

I thought to myself, *if only Sarah and Jane had known there's a better way to elicit affection and support from others*. If only they realized we all struggle with knowing what to say or do to comfort our loved ones, especially when we're frustrated. Had they known that people don't intentionally hold back care or affection from loved ones, that our love ones at times needs us to alleviate their doubts before they can give, things may have turned out differently for Sarah and Jane.

Partners can treat each other harshly and then justify it by saying one hurt the other first. But competing with loved ones over who is hurting worse merely traps us into relationships in which no one wins or feels secure. It's a race to the bottom. Win or lose, we end up hurt and frustrated with each other. When we try to win by proving we were right, it comes at the cost of trust, confidence, and respect. Our partners feel as if we are putting our need to be right above their feelings.

We hurt, so we blame, not realizing there might be no one to blame at all. Peter hadn't intentionally tried to hurt Sarah, nor would Sarah ever purposely try to hurt him, so why would she believe her loved one would have malicious intent toward her? She might believe this because she was holding flawed assumptions that blinded her to her partner's struggle. Like many of us, she was reacting to her fears and hurt, never questioning the assumptions that led her to make them.

Peter wanted to know he wasn't being blamed or criticized. If she had understood that, she would have reassured him that all she wanted was his support. In turn, he would have naturally wanted to comfort and reassure her. Instead, Sarah thought Peter was being defensive, not realizing her need to "win" had triggered his defensiveness. In the quest to "win," we plaster our loved ones with many negative labels such as - ungrateful, stupid, unattractive, useless, or other horrid things. Worse yet, we still expect them to accommodate our needs. And because they feel attacked and pressured, our loved ones become defiant and obstinate; and the more we push the more defensive they become. In our frustration, we call our loved ones spiteful names, and still expect them to give us what we want or need. No one wishes to be insulted and then be expected to comply. But this is what many of us do.

I have been on both sides – as the accuser and the accused. As the accuser, I expected others to know I care, and tolerate my insensitive words. Each time I belittled them or was not thoughtful about how I phrased things, it sowed seeds of doubt. Somewhere in their subconscious, my loved ones questioned my intentions and whether I cared or not. They may have intellectually known it but did not feel it. When I've been on the receiving end, I've been called many cruel names and frequently my defiance wasn't about whether I cared for them or not. Much of it was in response to the labels they plastered on me. I was called stupid, insensitive, arrogant, condescending, or mean, and felt that if I did complied with their demands or requests, it would somehow be admitting that those labels were true.

This cycle of hurt and misguided efforts to receive support all too often keep us from feeling acknowledged. And when we don't know how to elicit affection without making our partners feel attacked, we simply end up eliciting the treatment we're trying to avoid. When this happens, it's easy to perpetuate the false belief that our partners are the ones who are guilty of not caring for us, and that they really are hurtful and inconsiderate. Because we fail to realize this is not necessarily true and what we perceive is through our own window of pain, we end up experiencing this in relationships over and over again, and wonder why we struggle with our relationships. Rather than looking inward at our assumptions about others and relationships, all too often we strive mightily to change everything except ourselves, hoping this will improve things. But it doesn't - the same problems persist. We improve the packaging without delving into the contents — our beliefs and assumptions about the world, ourselves, and others.

The following are some truths that took me years to understand:

- The fear of being hurt is at the root of my relationship problems.

- My loved ones lash out because they're in the grip of fear and hurt and may need comforting (a sympathetic ear and heart).

- My partner's frustration is actually a plea for love, affection, and reassurance.

- My partner's defensiveness is a reflection of how I portray myself to him/her; my partner may need reassurance she/he is not being blamed when we share difficult truths.

- When I justify and defend myself, I belittle my partner, making him/her feel as though I've deemed him/her as "wrong."

> I can't always be right because I don't know everything; no one has infinite knowledge.

> My partner doesn't always understand because she/he has very different assumptions about the world than I do.

> Relationships are about easing each other's fears, not aggravating them.

> When my loved one tries to hurt me it's because she/he feels I'm trying to hurt them.

Knowing and operating from these truths has made the biggest difference in the quality of my relationships. Hopefully, they'll help you in yours. If only the old me, the fearful and defensive one, had known these things, and had the foresight to avoid all the hurts and angst. But life is not always that easy. Many of life's lessons are only learned in hindsight.

"My loved one's frustration with me is a plea for reassurance, an acknowledgment of his/her feelings and commitment to our relationship."

Chapter 4

Let Them Guide You

Sometimes, we can learn the best relationship lessons from our ex-partners and loved ones. They have much to teach us about ourselves when we're struggling, and experiencing perpetual relationship ruts. Upon reflecting how my fears and hurts were controlling me, I learned to ask for direction from loved ones. Even though I felt I knew, I asked anyway. It was quite a revelation. Learning to become a student to my loved ones allowed them to teach me about their fears and build my empathy and understanding.

There were plenty of ups and downs. One of the biggest lessons I learned was that when I assumed I knew or understood what my loved ones wanted from me, I was frequently wrong. I had a know-it-all attitude (about them), and in truth, I was far from knowing it all. I learned that the less I assumed about others the better. I also learned that without a mutual willingness to overcome the fear of being hurt, there simply can't be a strong connection with another person. Sometimes we need to forgo our own hurt to notice our loved ones are struggling with their own pain.

In many of my relationships, to protect from being hurt, I created an emotional shell around myself. This covering helped me pretend to be strong when all I was actually doing was numbing my feelings toward others, compensating for how fearful and fragile I was inside. In pretending to be strong all the time and trying to protect myself from being hurt, I ended up fooling everyone around me—including myself. Much of the bravado I exhibited was simply an attempt to keep others at arm's length. I acted aloof, nonchalant, indifferent, even defensive, and confrontational, but I wasn't sure why.

    I was trapped in a pattern of behavior I didn't know how to break until I finally realized that the fear of being hurt was the origin of my struggles. This one anxiety formed the basis for all. Whenever I broke down my various fears —fear of commitment, rejection, and abandonment, among others— they all came from an overwhelming desire to avoid being hurt.

    One dread led to another. Worrying I might be disappointed by others, I held my heart close to my chest, not letting others in and not expecting too much of others. If anyone dared get close to me, I often held back, subconsciously causing the relationship to dwindle and die. I was always testing my partners affection and commitment, but wasn't able to offer the essential security to them that I so desperately sought for myself. I knew my loved ones weren't sure where they stood with me or where our relationships were going. If it meant the possibility of being hurt, I was unwilling to ease their fears. This mindset caused my relationships to fall apart. I would tell myself it was my partner's fault, either because she didn't understand me or because we were incompatible, so I could exit from the relationship still intact. Yet, who *would* ever be able to truly understand me as long as I continued to fortify and maintain the wall of separation I had erected to keep myself from being hurt again?

Honestly, I was living a lie, perpetuating my own hurt without realizing it, and sacrificing long-term happiness by reacting to short-term fears. In trying to avoid being hurt, I became unlovable. Wanting to avoid pain, I became painful to interact with.

Does this sound like you, your partner, or someone else you know: being run by your fears of being hurt or rejected? Wanting (expecting) others to accept you for who you are, but struggling to accept them first? Wanting others to understand you before you attempt to understand them?

One big thing I had to learn was how a willingness to try and appreciate the other person first would ultimately help me move past these fears. The book, *The 5 Love Languages*, by Gary Chapman, gave me great insights, one of which is, when it comes to love, people feel it differently. An example I can draw from was something that plagued me with my ex-fiancé. For me, having space in the relationship and receiving words of affirmation were ways in which I felt loved. For her, she felt love through creating happy memories and spending "quality time" together. I was young and quite ambitious and needed the freedom to pursue my goals. It felt that no matter what I did, I was unable to meet her needs on a frequent enough basis. Her father had committed suicide when she was in grade school, which left her with fears of being abandoned. Every time I withdrew to focus on my work, it flared her insecurities and doubts. Because she didn't feel loved, she, in turn, withheld her affection and words of affirmation, which made me question if she loved me. Neither of us understood that how we feel and expressed love differed greatly.

When we think about it carefully, the word "love" itself is a fuzzy, hazy term. I have asked many people to share with me what they considered to be love and what made them feel loved, and I've received a variety of answers. Even though what they shared made sense, when I delved deeper, everything was still hazy and vague. If we all know what love is, why is it that so many of us struggle when showing it or sharing it with others?

In part we wrestle because we don't really sit down to think about how we "*feel*" love or how those we care about may experience love. We know how *we* interpret and experience love, but we don't consider what it means to our partners. We assume that our loved ones—and in fact, everyone—experience and expresses it similarly. It is this assumption which causes such grief.

Here are a few examples: For many women, when their partners do the dishes, help clean the house, or change a diaper, they see these actions as reflections of love for them. Thoughtfulness and partnership inside the home mean a lot more than all the flowers in the world. For some women, these expressions carry the same value that sex does for men. For a man, sex is required to make him feel loved by a woman. A man needs sex to feel connected to his partner; he needs it to feel reassured that she is still his. When she rejects his advances, he feels insecure and worries she may no longer desire him—not just that one night, but long-term. After enough rejections, a man starts to question whether his partner still loves him, sometimes even going as far as wondering if she may have found someone else.

At the heart of the issue is that all too often we assume we know what our loved ones want, based on what *we* want. And we assume our loved ones should just "know" what we want –what to do or say to make sure we feel loved. Rather than try to give love based on assumptions, we need to be willing to learn and then speak our partner's "love language." If we can do this, both partners' needs will be met.

We need to let them guide us – to tell us what they want and need to feel loved. Here is a useful exercise to get this guidance, and better understand your own love language as well.

LOVE ASSOCIATION EXERCISE

Complete the sentence below with at least five to ten different answers, and then compare them with the responses of your loved ones or friends. You'll start to see how similar and how different you might be in how you experience and express love or affection. For another point of comparison, my answers are found in the appendix.

I Feel Loved When You…

I Show My Love To You By…

I Love You For…

I Love The Fact That You…

    This exercise helps us gain a better understanding of how we experience love differently from our partner. When I did this with a partner, I realized I was oblivious to many things. I discovered the main reason my partners and other loved ones doubted me was because I kept giving them what *I* wanted without considering what it was *they* wanted. I was so busy expecting them to notice my efforts that I didn't realize they weren't feeling fulfilled, which left them with the sense that they were misunderstood and uncared for.

    Learning to show affection and love in ways others would appreciate seemed simple enough— but it was tough. It required more than just giving; it required me to deal with my fears and struggles. Before I could give others what they needed, I had to accept my own humility, ignorance, and shortcomings. I had to admit to myself that I didn't have all the answers and I had to be willing to acknowledge my ignorance and ask for direction and clarification. This was hard for me. I found, however, that I wasn't alone. Many others struggle with the same challenges.

Accepting that I could struggle at times made it easier for others to love me. It made it obvious for me to give them what they needed, rather than deciding what to give or assuming I knew better. Instead, I asked questions and allowed them to guide me. After all, they were on the receiving end.

Letting others decide what made them happy and fulfilled made things a lot less complicated. It made all the difference, and they felt loved and understood. I met their specific needs. Rather than stressing about whether or not I was doing the right thing, I let them tell me what they needed.

When I gave them what they wanted and needed, it was easier for me to make requests, so that my own needs could also be met. Not only were my loved ones more willing to listen, they were also more eager to accommodate. It takes some work to learn how to give each other what we want, but allowing one another to show the way to mutual satisfaction leads to far more hits than misses when giving and receiving love.

"Be willing to ask about your partner's

needs and wants—then satisfy them.

They decide how they feel;

we can only influence outcomes."

Chapter 5

We Seek What Affirms Us

When I was growing up, I had an overwhelming urge to prove how independent I was. I was determined to appear as if I didn't need to rely on others to achieve happiness or a sense of fulfillment. I wanted to demonstrate that I could take care of myself. Since I didn't want to burden others with my needs, I thought they shouldn't weigh me down with theirs. I was striving to be self-sufficient, so why shouldn't they do the same?

Does this sound familiar? Maybe you have a strong drive to be independent or know someone who isn't willing to rely on another person – the "I can do it myself" kind of attitude. If you're anything like how I used to be, you would rather struggle with hardship on your own than have to show your vulnerabilities to another person. But the more we strive to be independent and try to prove how capable we are, the more alone we feel.

In my relationships, I was so busy being independent, trying to prove I don't need others to love me, trying to prove I am lovable within myself, how I didn't need to rely on others, that I was unable to be vulnerable with my loved ones. It also made me unreceptive to affection. I found that the need to be independent sowed seeds of doubt and fear that I might leave the relationship, especially if I thought it would mean sacrificing my freedom.

Where did this need come from? Growing up, I felt as if I had to fight for everything. As I grew older, I thought others should have the same conviction, and the same emotional numbness as mine – this so-called independence. In truth, it wasn't independence – it was my unwillingness to accept my weaknesses. I had this insatiable need to feel like I was forging ahead. If I wasn't making progress in some way, it meant I was a failure.

It was when I was learning to accept myself that I realized this was not true. The process of self-acceptance also helped me learn to accept others. I began to realize that others need to feel they can contribute in a relationship, and the more we fight for our freedom and independence, the more they feel unappreciated and rejected. And if we don't do something about this, their doubts will start to grow and, at some point, reach a threshold. Although our partners may love us, they may wonder whether they can ever completely be happy in the relationship with us.

To have contentment in our relationships, there has to be a two-way affirmation. I used to believe this meant showing affection. But it's only half the picture. Being lovable isn't just about me giving to others; it's about being someone they want to give *to*, and becoming a worthy recipient of their affection. We need to learn to be that willing recipient, and help others feel that they are able to give. To be able to give and receive helps both parties feel recognized, appreciated, and valued, which in turn makes us feel loved.

Maybe the secret to a healthy lasting relationship isn't just about the willingness to show love, but also about us being ready recipients of others' affection. But how can we do this when striving for independence is so important to us? Where does this need for independence (and unwillingness to receive affection and support from others) come from?

With me, I always thought I had to be strong and impervious to fear, but there came a time when I realized this was not working for me. Although I'd convinced myself that being emotionally numb and keeping others at arm's length was a viable strategy, in truth, I was only running away from my fear of making myself vulnerable to another person.

Many of us hold back in our relationships, unwilling to become emotionally vested, or we expect too much from another person because we fear the relationship may one day end. With greater expectations of another person comes a greater chance we'll be hurt. If we assume from the beginning that we *will* eventually be hurt, then sooner or later, we will do our best to avoid becoming too emotionally involved in any relationship. We avoid letting others get close, in order to protect ourselves from becoming too attached to them in the first place.

By always assuming the worst we can subconsciously look for reasons to defend and argue, to justify why we should numb ourselves. This can lead us to being prone to perceiving criticism where none exists. As much as I wanted to be close to others, my expectation of being disappointed made it difficult for my partners to contribute to the relationship. Many times, I reacted negatively to their efforts even though I knew they meant well. This made them worried and tense around me, fearful I might retaliate. That's why they held back in the first place. I blamed them for their cold, uncaring, and nonchalant demeanor, but in the end, it was me who made them tense and unsure. It seemed they doubted me, too. And, in hindsight, they should have—I was giving awfully clear signals that I doubted our relationships could last.

  I used to believe you should never depend on others to have your best interests at heart because others are always too preoccupied with their own well-being. How can we trust others when there is always a chance they may turn on us and sacrifice our well-being if it happens to jeopardize theirs? We hold back, but then others doubt us because we doubt them. This creates a cycle of distrust. Breaking this cycle of hurting and distrusting each other takes a lot of courage. It is quite daunting to find out – how to break this cycle of hurt.

  The first step is learning to be emotionally present with ourselves and others. We need to realize how we may have unintentionally hurt our loved ones by not noticing what they may want to share with us. Frequently, distracted by our own thoughts, we can be incapable of being emotionally present with them. We may believe there are certain things they should be able to handle on their own, and get annoyed when we're approached with what seem (to us) to be trivial concerns. When they do approach us, we listen out of a sense of obligation, not out of desire, making them feel they're a burden, implicitly conveying that their feelings don't matter. I didn't realize my annoyance and my lack of enthusiasm for offering assistance was what stirred hurt in my partner. Layered inside what she wanted to share was a simple message: to share, to be heard, and to be supported.

In playing the independence card and thinking of others as being demanding or needy, I didn't realize how much I was casting doubts in others' minds with my words and actions. By being frequently frustrated with them, I made them doubt whether I would stick around. My striving for independence and freedom triggered their fears of being abandoned or that I might find someone else. This fear made them more demanding, needy and more prone to being jealous. Unsure of how much I was committed to them, if I was willing I was to stay with them, they tried to get me to commit more and tried to get me to prove how much I loved and wanted to be with them. To protect themselves, they would also start to emotionally hold back. They too, would start to assume the worst—that one day the relationship would end. And all this because I was busy being independent, assuming the worst, and in the process making that a self-fulfilling prophecy.

Instead, I needed to learn to take the tough armor off, and be willing to engage in the art of affirmation. This means opening our hearts, telling our loved how precious their presence is within our lives, and affirming that we want to be with them as much as they want to be with us.

*"It's not just about whether we're giving:

it's also about being someone

who is easy to give to."*

Chapter 6

The Price Tag of the Need to be Right

We've all been on the receiving end of a loved one's wrath. How did it make you feel? Did you argue back, or try to explain yourself, only to see it go awry and further fan their frustration?

We all want someone who accepts us, shortcomings and all. But every time our partners judge us, nag us, try to control, dominate, change, or manipulate us, it feels like they're telling us that we're not good enough. If we were good enough they wouldn't try to change us.

Maybe this isn't the case. It may feel like our partner is rejecting us. But it could also be their way of trying to get us to realize how we're hurting them. It isn't that they don't accept us—they are, after all, with us for a reason. It may just be that they want us to change our behavior, words, or actions because of deeper hurts or fears.

Imagine your partner constantly correcting you, justifying why you're wrong, or defending his/her own blamelessness. It doesn't feel good, does it? If anything, it feels downright awful. It's as if they are indirectly saying they don't care for your feelings. We come to them, trying to express how their words or actions are hurting us, but they're more focused on trying to point out ours and aren't willing to accept their role in our pain. It feels like a competition, tallying each other's shortcomings and wrongdoings.

We wouldn't want to be in a relationship with someone who neglects and disregards our feelings, someone who's more concerned about being right than letting us share our feelings. The frustration at each other might not be about who's right or wrong, rather a struggle of hurts. Every time we broach a subject that relates to how our partner may have hurt us, it can easily escalate into an argument. It's difficult to listen to others complain about their frustration with us, or about what we may have unknowingly or accidentally done. We can reflect back on how long we've been together, trying to recollect memories of sweet words of admiration, praise or appreciation. However, what seem to overflow in our memories are complaints, complaints, and more complaints. No one would want to stay in this type of relationship for long.

Sadly, sometimes we're so busy being right that we don't notice when we're wrong. We're too proud to admit our shortcomings or wrongdoings. Occasionally, what we argue about may not even be what they're complaining about. It might simply be a plea to make sure they still matter to us.

Some of us have such a strong need to be right because we feel we know better. This can make us obstinate, defensive, and proud. My need to be right caused me to argue with others, especially when I felt their argument somehow implied that I was wrong. I mistakenly interpreted their words as a judgment that I wasn't good enough. It's the notion that we have to be right that drives us to argue, defend, and thus unwilling to admit our faults. The need to be right might our desire to prove we're good enough, prove (to ourselves) that we're deserving of affection. The more we argue about how capable we are and how we don't require others' support, the more we end up pushing them away.

We all have the desire to contribute to the well-being of our loved ones and be reassured that we're capable of doing something right. This makes us feel that we matter to them. Although when we're too focused on being right, thinking we know better, they may feel we don't actually care about their input. When we're assuming we know what is good for them we may not be seeing their complaint for what it really is – that their opinions, their voice, are not being considered.

Where does the need to be right come from? Is it really the ultimate tragedy to be wrong, to admit our faults, or to say we're sorry? To be the first one to admit we've done wrong, but that we're dedicated to correcting our ways?

Being right didn't make me feel loved; it may have inflated my ego, but it didn't make another person want to be with me. I needed to realize that making my ego (and my need to boost it) more important than giving and receiving love was going to squelch any relationship. Taking the steps to be more caring about my loved ones' feeling heard and understood made all the difference. They needed to feel validated in the relationship with me, to know their input and their contribution to my well-being was being noticed, and that they had a right to choose what makes them happy.

No doubt about it, however, taking the first step to letting go of the need to be right can be hard. The difficulty ultimately lies in our fears of not being good enough. There's no need to take a giant leap; just by taking simple steps in the right direction, we can change everything for the better. Our efforts don't need to be on a grand scale. There are plenty of ways to begin: noticing when judgments about the other crop up inside us, and then looking within to grasp their origins, rather than making those judgments known. It can also take the form of showing appreciation, openly acknowledging our loved ones' attempts and the contributions they make to our lives, complimenting, listening intently as they talk about their day, or even be something as simple as writing a short love note. It could also manifest through swallowing our pride and asking for their help, or in seeking their advice. The more we learn to watch our own egos and restrain from reacting on our own insecurities, the more we will be able to love, and not have to judge those we love.

We all struggle with showing our vulnerabilities and sharing ourselves openly and honestly. When we struggle with our fears, we tend to hold back and be aloof and nonchalant because we don't want others to get too close, fearing they may discover how inadequate we may feel inside. We're scared others might find out how lacking, sad and lonely we may be feeling, how human we are, because they might leave us. This was very much how I felt. I thought I was being cautious and smart in how I was dealing with people and relationships. My opinion was the more I hide my vulnerabilities, the more likable I would become; sadly, it didn't work out that way. The more I tried to hide my vulnerabilities and insecurities, the more apparent they became. I thought I was being smart, but why were all my relationships struggling? Things only started to improve when I stopped trying to hide my vulnerabilities. Accepting that I had shortcomings and that we all struggle from time to time helped me free myself from the tight grasp that having to be right had on me.

It's an odd situation - the more we fight our fears, the more they control us. The more we accept them, the freer we become. This may seem completely counterintuitive, but it works.

For many of us, admitting and accepting our shortcomings is very difficult. What's even harder is the idea of sharing our fears and insecurities with others. We may worry that our inner turmoil might diminish the confidence, respect, and admiration others have for us. So rather than sharing it, we bottle it up. We hold it all in and let our doubts leak out in other ways.

In times of doubt, we can seek things that affirm our self-worth. We may look for them in the eyes of others, to remind ourselves we're lovable, that we're deserving of happiness and affection. We may throw ourselves into our work or our career, because this is where we feel we're somewhat more in control.

Doubts and insecurities aren't dirty words,

nor should we feel ashamed for having them. No one is immune to them. Everything in life comes as a bundled package. We're driven as much by our fears and insecurities as we are by our desires and confidence. When we move toward something new, we're easing away from something else. These are two sides of the same story and driving force. Like all emotions, there is a duality. On the one side, we want the best for our loved ones, while on the other side lay our pride and insecurities. The sooner we can see that we may be masking our fear of being wrong by thinking we're caring for our loved ones, the sooner we might be able to do something about it, like letting our loved ones be able to express themselves freely and fully.

Sometimes the need to be right might be what's blinding us from seeing things from our loved one's point of view. Not because we have malicious intent, but because we don't know better. The need to be right stops us from accepting humility, and opens us up to inadvertently hurting others without realizing it.

"It isn't about being right;

it's assuring them that their opinions

are heard."

Chapter 7

The Cornerstone of Relationships

Trust is the cornerstone of every relationship. Trust is the first thing we need for a relationship to grow; it's also very often at the heart of what gets questioned when we have an argument with a loved one. When we get hurt, when we feel that our loved one has betrayed our trust, it instills doubt within us. This ultimately makes us question whether or not our loved ones truly care for us.

Frequent lashing out is a common sign of a breakdown in trust. When relationships take on a defensive nature, the question of trust is raised, although maybe not in obvious ways. Each and every time we share, we implicitly ask the other, "Do I trust you enough to be open and honest?" Each time we hold back, we're implicitly asking, "Can I trust you with my vulnerabilities?" Every word and every action is laced with the question, "Can I trust you?"

When we hurt each other, we're sowing seeds of doubt. Every time we make an effort to make others feel cared for and understood we're sowing seeds of trust. Hopefully there will be sufficient trust sown so that, although we may be hurtful or may be hurt by them at times, we'll still be able to offer each other the benefit of the doubt. Perhaps they'll realize that, despite our carelessness when our words or actions injure them, much of it is simply an attempt to love them by sharing ourselves.

Even though we may want them to trust us enough to share, they may be struggling to do so. It may be because of something we've done or said that makes them doubt us. If this is the case, we have to figure out what the problem is and build up the foundation of trust again. Other times it may have to do with something within them and not necessarily with us having done wrong. Maybe it's an unresolved past hurt or some type of emotional baggage they aren't even aware of. We all have emotional baggage of some kind.

When it's an issue of personal emotional baggage, we need to figure out the root cause. Many times, it may be family related. For example, a parent leaving them when they were very young, or having to watch the two people they loved the most in the world (their parents) fighting and eventually go through a horrible divorce. It may be a past relationship struggle of theirs, a former partner who cheated on them leaving an emotional scar, making them fearful and paranoid about being abandoned again. It may have been a childhood trauma of being bullied and belittled by others, causing hurt that they keep bringing along into their relationships. Whatever the case may be, past hurts have taken root in their psyches, affecting how they react in relationships with partners, children, family, colleagues, friends, and even strangers.

Another example of emotional scars is being called stupid or having our intelligence questioned (due to consistently poor grades or someone we respect telling us we won't amount to much). Situations like this make us feel intellectually inferior. We become highly sensitive to words like, "idiot," "stupid," or "dumb." We have this constant need to react and defend ourselves all the time. Personally, I know how this feels because it's something I have struggled with most of my childhood and early adult life – and to be honest, still struggle with today.

    Much of my childhood, I carried the beliefs that I was unintelligent and unlovable, and because of this, I acted in ways that *made* me unlovable. I had such an urge to boast, show-off, or prove how knowledgeable or intelligent I was that I came across as arrogant or condescending. Much of my boasting and showing off was an attempt to get others to validate my intelligence. I looked for external validation because I wasn't so sure of it within myself. Frequently, I boasted because I was so proud of the goals I had achieved. It wasn't because I thought highly of myself, but because many years earlier I doubted I would ever achieve even a fraction of those same goals.

    This need to brag, this need to seek other's acceptance and admiration was a nasty habit and belief that didn't just disappear overnight. The more I became aware of it, the more I was able to confront it for what it was – a need to prove, an insecurity I was trying to cover up that at times rubbed people the wrong way.

    Insecurities like this go back to my struggle to learn to speak and write. When it comes to the English language, I was a late bloomer. I had been quietly embarrassed and ashamed of the fact that I did not utter my first word until the age of five and my parents were fearful that I might have been mute. It may have been the result of being in a foreign country, in a refugee camp for the first four years of my life where there wasn't really any stable language because I lived in a smorgasbord of cultures. It might have been because I was socially awkward or the byproduct of growing up in a bilingual community where broken English was the norm. It might have been because in the household I grew up in you were *spoken to* as a child. Whatever the reason, I left high school with a stunted vocabulary and poor grasp of the English language. I always compared myself to others and felt inadequate in some way.

Despite these challenges, as well as not studying much in high school, I was still able to get into University. It wasn't long before I realized how far behind I was in how I spoke and wrote. There was a lot of catching up to do in my overall wealth of knowledge, even for the most basic courses. It was quite disheartening, but the feeling of lack actually spurred me on. As a result, I sat at the local library almost every evening for the next few years learning. The first book I read was *The Seven Habits of Highly Effective People* by Stephen R. Covey. This book was also the beginning of my love affair with self-help books and personal development.

There I was, feeling out of place, incompetent and fake, reading books with a dictionary in one hand and a pen in the other. As I read, I underlined words I did not understand, looked them up in the dictionary, and wrote down the definitions. I did this for a few years. However dealing with family problems at home and overcoming my writing and reading shortcoming, my studies proved to be more of a challenge than I could handle. My grades started dropping like a stone in a pond. Eventually I ended up quitting college and floating through the first years of my adult life trying to figure out where I wanted to go from there. Struggling with how to get back on track reinforced my feelings of stupidity and lack and my belief that I might not amount to much in life.

It was clear I needed help and so I went out of my way to find role models in people in history books and self-help books. I ended up reading hundreds of books, frequently two or three times to get the gist of the message. It has taken time, but I have also worked hard on my speaking and writing skills, which has helped heal this trauma in my life.

We all have our own set of traumas, and it is through these traumas and past experiences that areas of oversensitivity are created inside us. They can so easily become areas we defend the most, as we are unable to trust anyone with because we're doubtful of it ourselves. Having a simple, straightforward explanation of which among the traumas can cause which hurts and fears can help us greatly. Below is my attempt at linking possible fears with past hurtful experiences. They may not always be accurate, but offer a better understanding of where distrust may stem from.

Being bullied – instills a common distrust among people in general. Bullying makes us antagonistic and prone to misinterpreting neutral statements as hostile. We become more aggressive toward others. When you've been bullied, the fear of being hurt lingers on into adulthood. It makes us struggle with showing affection, tolerance, love, or compassion to others, mainly because we feel it wasn't shown to us in the first place. We approach the world with the idea that it's best to attack and reject others before they have a chance to attack and reject us. We become so busy defending and attacking that we can't stop; it's is ingrained in us. We often attack those we love most.

At times it could have the opposite effect. We may start to question our own self-worth because we feel at fault for the struggles and anguish of others – especially when it involves a loved one. We feel we're the problem, so we take much more hurt upon ourselves and become tolerant to abuse and misuse. We allow ourselves to become victims and emotional punching bags because we don't feel we're worthy of love, even though we may desperately yearn for it and want it. We feel we deserve the hurt we receive.

<u>When our parents' divorce</u> – it can make us question whether marriages can really work. We question whether there will ever be a "happily ever after" for us and we become fearful of commitment. Even though we may want to believe in fairy tales and the idea of "happily ever after," we tend to look for reasons to bail out of relationships whenever anything starts getting too serious. For some of us, when our parents get divorced, it can instill a need for independence; we feel a need to fight and protect our sense of freedom, not realizing that we're reacting to a past trauma. It's not that we don't want

a relationship; it is because we don't want to confront the possibility of giving our all in a relationship only to end up broken hearted, and confirming our belief that all marriages ruin relationships.

Poor academic achievements – can make us question our intelligence. We develop an intellectual inferiority complex, and become overly sensitive when people question our abilities. This tendency drives many of us to pretend that we know more than we actually do and to defend our views. It can also make us stubbornly defiant, despite knowing we may wrong. It makes many of us unwilling to ask for guidance or help, rendering us unable to acknowledge our ignorance, making us come across as arrogant or obstinate, all in an attempt to avoid the feeling of being stupid.

Financial difficulties – can lead us to become doubtful of our future. Money problems can make us feel the need to save and scrimp, or to become frustrated with our partners' or family members' spending habits. This can also turn into depriving ourselves and our loved ones of life's little luxuries.

There's another side to feeling deprived of life's luxuries. Because our families suffered so much financially or because we felt deprived as children, comparing our clothes and toys with those of our peers and classmates, we can feel the need later in life to get high status jobs and earn huge amounts of money to buy all the things that should compensate for the deprivations of our childhood. Many of us end up in jobs we despise to provide our loved ones with the luxuries we didn't get as children. Some of us can find it hard to control impulsive buying habits even as we fall deeper and deeper into debt because of entrenched fears and hurts that make us feel deprived and suffocated. Some people hoard, becoming stingy and tight with money; others feel the need to spend and splurge to overcompensate for deprived childhoods.

Our current relationship struggles – can include feelings of guilt toward our loved ones. Maybe we have children and our partner seems absent or unwilling assist in co-parenting. We may feel guilt toward our children and experience the need to compensate for the void left by our partner by spoiling them with material things or not being as strict as we should. Much of this is an attempt to ease our own guilty feelings of being unable to give them two parents.

Past relationship hurts (1) – Depending on past relationship hurts, the way we approach our next relationships will be different. If we were at fault, for example, we've wronged our past partners in some way (resulting in the break up) we may become prone to guilt, making us more willing to sacrifice our own well-being to make our current relationship work more successfully than our past relationships.

Past relationship hurts (2) – If our ex-partner betrayed us in some way, we may inadvertently make our current partner a scapegoat for our ex-partner's crimes. For example, if our ex-partner cheated on us, we may become much more fearful of our current relationship that it results in us becoming too clingy, needy, and easily jealous of others as we are more prone to feeling neglected, mistreated, and misunderstood.

Past relationship hurts (3) – We may have felt so betrayed in past relationships that we have (consciously or subconsciously) made the decision that we cannot trust anyone again. Since we've become suspicious of everyone, even our current partners, we're unable to be there for them emotionally. Instead of sharing ourselves openly and honestly, we create an emotional wall around our hearts, acting cold, nonchalant and aloof, pretending that others cannot hurt us – when in truth, we're very fearful and sensitive to their words. We would rather not let others know how much they affect us. We may feel that each and every time we share we always get hurt, so we decide that it may be best to just not let others in at all, since we feel it will only lead to further pain.

These are some examples of how past pain may be causing current problems in our personal or professional relationships. Hurt is pervasive; we all struggle with a unique mix of former painful experiences. Some experiences are more traumatic than others, but they all affect us. Previous hurts are insidious; even though we may not believe or think they still affect us - they do. In truth, they always will affect us, that is, until and unless we become willing to accept their existence and confront the hurt we feel. Denying old hurts will only allow it to grow in strength, controlling and infecting new relationships we enter.

Trust is hard to build in relationships without looking at ourselves and our past hurts. Taking steps to build trust can be daunting, especially for those who struggle with trusting others in the first place. We need to realize that our distrust of others may not be warranted at all. Instead it may be an unresolved past hurt of ours, and we may be unknowingly making our partner the scapegoat.

When fear and hurt are what we're accustomed to, frustration and antagonism is what we expect from others. When we're already guarded and defensive, expecting to be hurt and betrayed, we push our loved ones away with our actions and words without realizing it. Learning not to do this and learning to trust instead takes effort. At times it can feel impossible because it just feels too hard to take the initiative to share ourselves openly and let others in. It is easier to expect others to take the initiative, and to prove to us that they are trustworthy. Even if they do, no matter how much they try, we can still be fearful and unable to let down our guard. We can still feel unsure about trusting them. Similarly, we can believe that we should accept others only if they accept us first, and that it's our loves ones' responsibility to ease our fear, show us love and tolerate our insensitivity even though we struggle giving them the same trust in return.

Does the above sound like it would be successful—both parties waiting and wanting the other to share, neither agreeing to go first? No one wants to be the first to get hurt, so no one bothers to give first. When we hurt and feel attacked, we apportion blame. We point fingers at our partners, thinking they are emotionally underdeveloped or insensitive, not realizing that our partners are pointing their fingers at us. So who's being insensitive? We both are. We're both to blame, but neither seems willing to accept the responsibility, so neither ends up being fulfilled.

When hurting is all we know, fear is the only thing we understand. How do we begin to trust each other? How do we build the foundations of trust that are necessary in any healthy, emotionally rewarding relationship? A first step is to change our approach to relationships. All too often if we are feeling unlovable, we come to relationships with a focus on taking before giving love. If our partners are doing the same, then both parties try to take from the relationship and from each other, and there is no one left who's willing to give.

We need to take turns. For this to occur, we need to look into why we would ever approach relationships with the intention of *taking*, of being loved and fulfilled by another to begin with. This may be because we approach relationships with a *"scarcity mentality,"* or what is also known as the *"me first" syndrome.* When we expect others to prove they love us first before we give, we tend to believe there is a limited amount of love and affection available to us. The result: we neglect and attack our loved ones when they try to take from us, before we've had the opportunity to have our fill. No matter how much they seem to try, we always seem to never have enough love. And when it is our turn to give, we struggle because we don't feel they love us. And possibly no amount of affection would make us feel it.

Past hurts can lead us to have an insatiable

void within us. They can be quite devastating and affect us in many ways. It can lead us to protect ourselves in our relationships by seeking to have our needs fulfilled first. But in the end it only causes more pain. What happens when both people take and there's no one available to give? The relationship will not last.

There's another way. It's harder, but far more rewarding in the long run. It's when we approach relationships by looking for ways to be of service to each other. Finding ways to fulfill our partners' needs, finding out where their sense of scarcity stems from, what past hurts are being triggered and then giving first, even when we feel we have nothing to give. It requires us to acknowledge that our loved ones have their own set of needs and hurts. When we give first, we create a sense of abundance. This helps erase our partners' fears that there might not be anything left for them.

Many people feel revolted when they hear the terms "subservient" and "submissive," and confuse and misuse these words so much that they cause emotional reactions of disgust. For example we often hear men say they want a submissive woman; in truth, what they may really want is a partner who doesn't belittle them. Most of us don't really want submissive partners who always agree with us, or who will never express their feelings or wants, or are willing to be treated poorly. We want to feel that others are able to freely express their needs, to feel we are doing right by them. Just some of us confuse "submissive" for "supportive".

On the flipside, there is the misconception

that our partners want us to be doormats, that we should forego our needs to satisfy theirs. We frequently perpetuate this myth when we have to "show who's boss," show who's in control, or when we manipulate our partners into giving in to us. We don't realize that all we really want is to feel safe when we share with each other. It's a simple case of lack of trust, but we confuse it with a game of control and dominance.

It was through learning to be the one who trusts first, and to be trustworthy, that my relationships started to improve. Learning to be trustworthy is difficult, no matter what stage of emotional maturity we're at. It is an uphill battle because we aren't the ones who determine whether we succeed. Our loved ones determine whether we're trustworthy. Trust must take root in the mind of the other. This is very much the same idea as being a good partner, parent, employee, child, or friend. It isn't for us to determine whether we're succeeding; our relationship determines this. At times, we'll be great in one role but struggle in another.

Before we take the first step in becoming trustworthy, we need to figure out why we may be considered untrustworthy. We need to ask for feedback, accept our shortcomings and failings, and understand why others feel the way they do about us. We need to explain why we're trying to become more trustworthy and let our loved ones know that we struggle at times in proving why they should trust us. It isn't about getting it right all the time. It's about building a habit and striving for it that matters more than anything. We learn to become more trustworthy over time. Others begin to feel they can share more with us—and vice-versa.

How could we start overcoming and confronting fears and past hurts? First, find a place where you can be alone, feel safe, and free from distraction. Write down all of your past hurts. Recall and write down what happened, how you felt at the time, and what it meant to you. Write your thoughts about how it may have affected your life and your relationships up until now.

This can be quite confronting. When I did this, it allowed me to explore the many hurts controlling me. I avoided confronting and coming to terms with them, not realizing they were holding me captive without me knowing it.

Then gather the courage to find someone you trust most and share one or two of these painful experiences. Tell him/her what you want to do, and that you want him/her to help you explore a past hurt so you can overcome it. Request that s/he just listen, and not to interject or interrupt you while you share. Let him/her know you just want him/her to listen and nothing more, giving you a sympathetic ear.

Below is a way to structure your "hurt list" for this exercise.

➢ State what happened.

➢ How did you feel as a result?

➢ How you have interpreted what it meant?

➢ How it might be affecting you in your life and

relationships?

➢ Possible things you are doing to avoid re-experiencing similar past hurt.

➢ What would it mean if you could change, for you and for the relationship?

➢ What are steps you could take to steer yourself in the right direction?

If you do this for each hurtful experience, it can be a powerful process to build your trust with others and with yourself. Remember, there will always be times when we struggle and fail. Like with all healing processes, it's normal; it's a natural part of the learning and growing process. Over time, accepting the "two steps forward, one step back" dance becomes second nature.

"Trust is something you earn,

not something you should expect."

Chapter 8

What We All Seek

We all want to know we're loved and accepted for who we are. When others accept us completely, it means they don't try to change us; to tweak us to become perfect in their eyes, or change us so much that we end up losing sight of who we really are. We need to let others know we're growing and changing at our own pace, sometimes slower when we feel insecure, other times with great leaps when we feel invincible. Some days we feel it's tough; other days there's nothing to worry about. It's a bit of a rollercoaster.

But when we feel our loved ones are trying to push us to change (instead of nurturing and encouraging us), they seem to be implying that we're not good enough. Feelings of self-doubt increase and we start to wonder whether we're worthy of their love. If we are, then why do they seem to be so disappointed in us? Why is it that, no matter what we do, it never seems to be good enough?

Feeling criticized for who you are hurts and frustrates everyone. No one wants to be on the receiving end, yet too many of us happily dish it out, belittling our loved ones for perceived shortcomings. The fact that our partners stay with us is a fairly solid sign that they love us enough. They wouldn't stay if they didn't. However, when they belittle us, we feel rejected, if they loved us for who we are, they wouldn't feel the need to tell us what we need to change and what we're doing wrong.

At times, we may the one trying to change the behavior of a loved one. We see them doing something we feel may be destructive, possibly hurtful, and we can't help wanting to steer them away from it. It isn't that we are trying to change them (even if it comes across that way), we only want to change a part of their behavior, to see what we do and realize that it is as much for their welfare as it is our own.

Growing up, my parents went through many bouts of trying to change the other. This led to arguments that often escalated yet having the same theme over and over again. Based on what I saw with my parents, I grew up thinking that criticism, anger, bitterness, resentment, and frustration were normal and common themes in all relationships. Despite promising myself I would never be like them, I ended up emulating my parents' relationship in many ways.

And one of those ways was being critical of my loved ones. Many of us don't realize how much we may push our loved ones away when we criticize them. Even when they tell us we're being this way, their pleas fall on deaf ears because we're unwilling or unable to understand their point of view. Maybe this is because we resent them for past hurts, or because we're so intent on getting our point across that we're slowly killing the rapport we so enjoyed at the outset of the relationship.

Loving others doesn't mean pushing our way into their lives. It's about letting them know how their actions impact us, letting them know when they're triggering our own past painful experiences, which make us fearful and worried about the relationship. We're only asking them to realize how much they're adversely affecting us. How their actions may make us question their appreciation and acceptance of us.

It's hard to restrain ourselves when we feel our loved ones are doing something that may hurt them, or us. We can't help but intervene, hoping they'll see our efforts as a result of our concern for them. Instead of being grateful for our efforts, they may become frustrated or angry with the one who cares most about them.

As much as we try to help, it sometimes backfires. Even when what we want is reasonable, even if what we're saying is true and for their benefit, maybe we're creating the barrier we're experiencing. Perhaps their defensiveness and stubbornness is born out of a sheer desire to protect themselves, not out of the need to justify or defend their actions, but who they are as a person. When we try to change someone's behavior, the thoughts that run through his/her mind turn to doubts about whether we accept him/her and/or notice their individuality and value.

People will agree to change and grow as long as we enable them to preserve their sense of identity. Let them know their growth in one area doesn't need to come at the cost of anything else that's precious to them. By accepting them and recognizing their individual needs and expectations, they won't feel the sting of rejection because they'll feel as though the change is a request and an opportunity for them, rather than a threat to their identity.

Partners want to know they're accepted for who they are and that we love them despite their eccentricities and quirks. Letting them know we fell in love with them because of some of their peculiarities is a huge step forward because it tells them we value them as a whole along with their unique ways.

Falling for others' unique qualities may seem like a strange phenomenon. We're somewhat different and yet intrigued by our respective peculiarities. But when we get into a relationship, we can start to feel a desire to change or improve the other person. We fall for our loved ones as they are, yet we then ruin everything by ending up trying to tweak them.

It's our differences that let us explore new facets of life and new experiences we wouldn't have been exposed to otherwise. It seems easy enough to understand and realize how important it is to accept another's uniqueness, but how do we do it?

We can begin by acknowledging our loved ones' individuality. What among their traits and beliefs do we respect and appreciate? Rather than trying to point out why our beliefs are right and why theirs are wrong, maybe we should just let them be. We wouldn't want our partners to compare us to one of their ex-partners, or our parents comparing us to another's children, why should we do that to our loved ones? Even though we may know that, we could have done or said things that gave them that impression. Maybe they love sports or other activities; taking this away would strip their source of joy. Perhaps we got frustrated at them for spending more time on their hobby instead of being with us. We wouldn't want our loved ones taking away our sources of pleasure (as long as they're fulfilling and healthy) so why would we demand the same from them?

However, there comes a time when we may want to ask the other to change. For example, early in our relationships we're often doting and eager to please. But as we get comfortable in our relationship, we can become a bit lax with our words and actions, or expect our loved ones to be more accepting of our insensitivities. We can start to feel as though our partners are taking our feelings for granted or aren't being as considerate of our well-being as they should be. We still appreciate their uniqueness and their quirks; it's just that at times, we have to ask them to be more aware of their words and actions, and how those things make us feel.

As the relationship progresses, it's possible that some of their quirks might hurt us. Because we're more comfortable, we can be more confident in requesting they change certain habits, not because we are rejecting them. Rather, it's because some of their habits might hurt us in some way. When we talk to them, it is crucial that we first acknowledge them; by reassuring them we are not rejecting them. This helps break down their resistance and emotional barriers. When asking for a change, by sharing our feelings, explaining how their actions hurt us, and why we want them to change, it leaves them empowered, not withdrawn. And, if they should accept our request, it's so important to express to them gratitude for accommodating our needs, and their desire to care for us.

We all fumble at times when trying to address our needs, when conveying to loved ones that what we need is to feel loved. Here are some ways to approach a loved one without hurting their feelings

Own the hurt – Explain why we feel frustrated and hurt, although not in a way that makes our loved ones feel as if they're being blamed.

Here are a few examples of a request as opposed to an accusatory statement. Learn to ask and not to blame. Blame causes defensiveness, stubbornness and at times, refusal to admit their faults. If we want our loved ones to notice and accommodate us, blaming is the worst thing we can do.

➢ *You're always out with your friends; you never spend time with me.* – We're blaming them for neglecting us and the relationship.

Instead: *I feel like you don't care for me. I know you do; I just feel neglected at times.* – A request for a loved one to be aware of our feelings of neglect.

➢ *Why can't you make an effort on my birthday?* – This feels like an attack, making them feel guilty.

Instead: *I'd like to go somewhere nice for our anniversary, somewhere special; do you have any ideas?* – A request to spend quality time with each other.

➢ *Why do you always have to spend money? You don't appreciate its value* – It feels like we're blaming them for financial problems.

Instead: *I'm worried we may not have enough for this month's bills and I'm not sure if we'll be able to save up enough for this year's holiday.* – Sharing our concerns while letting them know we need their assistance to save for something important.

➢ *Why do you always have to argue? Why can't you just do what I ask?* – We're blaming them for our relationship problems, making them the culprits of our hurt and frustration.

Instead: *Hun, can you just do this for me. I'm stressed out and don't have the energy to explain, but please just go along with it.* –Letting them know how we're feeling, while explaining this is a request, not a demand.

➢ *You're an emotional retard; you never do*

anything for me. All you ever do is take. –We're accusing them of being selfish, inconsiderate and degrading them by calling them names.

Instead: *I appreciate what you've done. I really do, I can see the effort you're making to love me. It's just that, at times I prefer you to do...* - Acknowledging them and their efforts while letting them know we want something else. Phrased this way, our request doesn't leave them feeling unappreciated or ridiculed for failing.

Give credit – Rather than stating what we've done and why we should be loved and acknowledged, instead let our loved ones feel the reward. Why are we hogging all the recognition when our loved ones may also be in need of it?

When we take credit for results, what we also convey is a lack of gratitude and appreciation for the contributions of others rather than realizing that a relationship, parenting, or any endeavor is a team effort. When we hog recognition without acknowledging others, it makes them feel unappreciated. Make them feel special, just in case they don't receive recognition for their efforts. By giving them recognition before our own they'll feel the desire to recognize our efforts.

Build trust – To dissolve their fear, build up their trust. To stop them from hurting us, figure out why they don't trust us in the first place. Ask for feedback and let them know we have their well-being at heart. Allowing them to share will build up their trust so they'll feel they can share anything and everything and we'll still accept them. Avoid comments that might sound like criticism or judgments.

Praise their failings – Appreciate any effort or attempts as gestures of their love. This will help instill the courage and confidence to try again. Criticizing their failure will only compound their fear and they'll be unwilling to try again, to avoid the hurt.

Our loved ones often want to give us what we want, but rather than show appreciation, we often make them feel criticized. It may not have been our intention; all we are trying to do is to convey what we want and how they can improve next time. The way we respond can leave them feeling criticized or encouraged.

The difference is subtle, but there's power in subtleties – the simple rewording of a phrase can change its impact for good or for bad, depending on how the sentence is structured, the words that are chosen, and the tone in which they are stated.

"We fall for each other for who we are, only to ruin it by trying to tweak things that aren't important."

Chapter 9

Freedom to Breathe

When we feel overwhelmed by our loved ones' demands, it's usually a sign we need to take time for ourselves and/or spend some time in recovery. What we think of as being someone else's fault may be symptoms of self-neglect. We feel ignored when we're too busy living life, trying to make ends meet, worrying about studies, losing sleep rearing a child, cleaning the house, or caring for an elderly parent. We forget to take a step back from it all and to care for the care-giver.

I believed that to be a good son, brother, or partner required me to be selfless, but being unselfish was hard, especially when I didn't feel I had much left of myself to begin with. The more I tried to be there for others without making an effort to care for myself, the more frustrated and withdrawn I became. There was a crucial puzzle piece missing, and had I stayed on that path, it would have led to resentment that will slowly build up over time. After a while I discovered it wasn't just about me being selfless (caring for others before myself), but being able to take care of myself without feeling guilty.

When we feel drained and exhausted, we should give ourselves permission to pamper and care for ourselves, and our loved ones should encourage us to do this. Being in a fulfilling relationship isn't about giving away every ounce of ourselves every second of every day. When we do this, we end up taking from our partners in other ways. This is something many of us struggle with. We reach a point where we're so depleted and frustrated that we unknowingly start thinking differently, in ways that cause us to end up questioning our relationships with loved ones.

    We all occasionally go through moments of frustration and feeling unloved. Feeling suffocated in our relationships from time to time doesn't make us bad people. We shouldn't feel ashamed for believing that our loved ones are taking too much from us. On the same note, just because we feel that way doesn't mean our loved ones are trying to take more or are demanding. It may simply mean we aren't spending enough time caring for ourselves. The assumption that another is taking too much of us can be due to the fact that we feel we have so little to give, or to share in the first place. We may feel we lack something.

    If we don't take a little time to care for ourselves, we have nothing to give when our loved ones come to us with their hearts' open. They will walk away hurting because we're so desperately trying to preserve what little we have left. When we burn ourselves out, we end up having so little left to give that we feel their needs and wants are heavier than ours. We may sense that they're being demanding or needy but it may be due to the reality that we're not taking enough time to care for ourselves.

We all know how it feels to be exhausted, drained from a grueling day at work, but how many of us can see it completely from our loved ones' perspective? How many of us make the effort to ease their load? They too may be nearing the breaking point, but when we're exhausted, tired, or frustrated we underestimate the load of their responsibilities. Most of the efforts our partners make to contribute to our well-being are frequently made when we're not watching, like working at a job they dislike to ensure the mortgage is paid on time, or cleaning the house so we can come home to a relaxing environment. We come home tired so we don't notice that they're in the same depleted state we are.

Many of us burn ourselves out emotionally throughout the day and when we come home, we turn to our partner not with the intention of giving, but waiting to receive because we're drained. In being unable to care for ourselves, or to get away from work and other commitments, we become dependent on our partners to make us feel loved. By failing to treat ourselves kindly, we saddle them with the responsibility to do so. We come to them empty, waiting for those in our lives to give, and then we get frustrated when they don't. We're sometimes incapable of realizing that they, too, are running on empty.

We need to recognize that at times both partners in the relationship will need some space. And sometimes we'll need to act on their behalf and pamper them because they can't do it themselves during low-energy moments.

"Gift of Space: let them take care of themselves without feeling guilty."

Many of us feel we should be constantly selfless, always giving our all to our loved ones. We may feel obligated to be there for them but at times, we do so at the cost of not caring for ourselves. When we focus on ensuring our loved ones are cared for, it means not doing something else. Whether it's walking in the park, snuggling on a comfortable sofa, or reading a good book in the corner of a café, we give up other opportunities. When we're working hard building a home, there'll always be something that demands our attention. When we're constantly distracted by other commitments, we can occasionally neglect our partners or ourselves. Sometimes we do this so much it causes the quality of our relationship to dwindle. Before we know it, we start to treat our partners as enemies, as sources of pain or barriers to our happiness.

When we strive to build a loving family we must forego something else. This can cause us to mourn our lost freedom. Feeling daunted and burdened by the responsibility of being a parent and caring partner is nothing to be ashamed of. But we do need time to focus on our needs —to be "selfish" (for sanity's sake) and not feel guilty about it. It's all right to take a time out to occasionally pamper yourself, because pampering yourself is not really being selfish. If we don't care for ourselves, how are we going to have enough to give?

Too many of us take for granted the therapeutic effects of spending a little time alone. In caring for ourselves we are replenished and so we gain greater abundance so we can give to others. By neglecting and sacrificing our own well-being, our loved ones experience less tolerance, compassion, and understanding from us. Loving others is very much about learning to love ourselves, too.

For me, there were times when I needed to get away from my family, but not because I didn't care for and love them. I was simply *unable* to be there for them because I was struggling with my own needs and frustrations. I couldn't give when there was nothing left to offer. When I started to realize that feeling unloved was actually about me not spending time to care for myself, I started revamping the relationship I had with myself. While objectively witnessing how I treated myself, it dawned on me that I needed some space to regain my composure. I was so busy pushing myself, trying to prove how worthy I was to others, seeking the admiration and adoration of others, that I never really bothered to spend time to find my own. Wanting the acceptance of others was a compensation for the lack of self-acceptance. I was in a race against myself and felt if I stopped, everything around me would crumble. I didn't want to slow down because that meant I would have to face and come to terms with the resentment and frustration bubbling inside me.

Every day was a battle, I was always trying to forge ahead but taking a break from it all was exactly what I needed most: time alone to think, to find out why I strove so hard, and why my tolerance of others was so fickle. I needed space to regain my thoughts and learn to treat myself better. How could I expect others to love me when I was constantly depleting myself to the point that I had so little left to give? How could I expect to love others effectively?

No one wants to be with partners who come to them empty, who always take before giving, or who always expect others to share first before they start giving. Partners who there are always frustrated and need others to be the givers are actually people who constantly treat themselves poorly on a regular basis. And in a relationship, partners who treat themselves poorly will frequently be the ones who take, because they're always running on empty. They won't have much to give because they're constantly depleting their own energies.

At the time, I was an emotional black hole. I spoke poorly in my head about myself, always held impossible expectations, and demanded so much of myself that I was constantly irritated. Frequently, I wasn't actually irritated with others, but at my own lack of accomplishments and my failure to follow through. Ultimately though, my frustration flowed outward onto others. I constantly dumped on my loved ones because I was constantly dumping on myself. I couldn't give others the love and tolerance they needed because I wasn't able to give it to myself.

It's difficult to make people feel fulfilled when we're an emotional black hole continually treating ourselves poorly. I gave to myself with one hand, without realizing I was taking with the other. No matter how much affection someone gave me, no matter how much time I spent trying to care for myself, it was an uphill struggle because I always took from myself in other ways. I treated myself so poorly that by the end of the day, I was left where I started: empty.

As I look at past relationships and those that surrounded me, I can see that we all struggle with finding time for ourselves. Sometimes we need our partners and loved ones to intervene. Helping us with the dishes, chores, or just encouraging us to take some time for ourselves, can do wonders to our relationship. Sometimes we need them to allow us be alone for a few hours—maybe a couple of days or even a week—while they take care of everything. We need our loved ones to give us space so we can recompose or focus on something we've been neglecting. We want to feel it's all right to take better care of ourselves, and when we're overwhelmed and drained, the people who love us allow us to recover and return to our loving selves once more.

We want our loved ones to share more, but they'll be unable to do that if they're constantly drained, as well. There must be a willingness on our part to shoulder more of the load from time to time. When they come home and we can tell they are overwhelmed, drained, or frustrated, they may need us to step in. Taking them out on a date, getting home early to spare them from doing the laundry, washing the dishes, cooking dinner or just cleaning the house so they can take a nap, are some of the simple things we can do. The effort doesn't need to be grand or costly, but it needs to exist. It's the constant caring response that makes a huge difference to a loved one's well-being. By taking on more responsibilities, we enable them to take time to appreciate themselves so they'll return to us replenished and with a sense of being able to contribute again. If we're unsure what to do, simply offering assistance as needed, or giving them space to breathe and think, can make a huge difference. Provide the space your loved ones need to appreciate themselves.

If we aren't willing to do this, our loved ones may reclaim space in other ways—by withdrawing their love – withholding sex or affection – because they feel we're doing the same thing. They may become unwilling to compromise or accommodate our needs in an attempt to preserve what little they may have left of themselves. None of us can give when we feel empty and depleted. When we don't give them space by finding simple ways to ease their burdens, they might take it out in less healthy ways.

We all need our own space and free time. Take what you need to fill yourself up, and don't forget that your partner needs to do the same. To be more present in our relationships, to be more giving, we need to let them cultivate their sense of self to feel fulfilled. For them to give more to us, we need to let them have time to cultivate themselves. They can't give what they don't have.

"Giving yourself and your loved ones the chance to replenish themselves creates the room and space to be able to give."

Chapter 10

In Search of Security

As we leave childhood behind, we start to identify ourselves with being separate from others: our parents, friends, and siblings. It takes time to etch out this sense of individuality and, at times, we'll go to great lengths to protect it. As we grow older and start to form intimate adult relationships, some of us become fearful of commitment, holding back from getting into things too quickly or too seriously. We string our partners along, always ending relationships when they get too serious or when things get too complicated.

Some people call this fear of commitment. I prefer to call it fear of losing oneself. Some of us hold back, because we start to feel our individuality is being jeopardized, it feels as if we're sacrificing what makes us happy to accommodate the needs of our partner.

The fear of losing my sense of identity made me recoil and withdraw from relationships altogether. I felt as though I had to abandon a bit of myself to make my partners happy and I was not okay with that. I felt I had to forego what fulfilled me to ensure that they were cared for, but each time I did this, a seed of resentment germinated. It seemed that every accommodation I made came at the cost of losing a bit of myself — until I eventually felt lost within the relationship.

At times, this fear or unwillingness to commit might be the result of a simple conflict of needs. Our partners might want to know where they stand with us, if we intend to be with them in the long term or not, while we want to know if we'll remain ourselves and not lose our sense of self — what makes us individuals — while we're in the relationship. Most of this running away from commitment might be their way of preserving their freedom or sense of individuality. Maybe the way to get them to commit more, moving to the next stage of the relationship, is to ease their doubts and worries.

As I look at others' relationships—those who aren't willing to commit and those who always seem to be stringing their partner along—it seems much of their reluctance is due to being unsure of their partners. The doubts they have about commitment are fundamentally about being accepted and making sure their individuality will be preserved. While observing relationships that seem to last, much of their success appears to be in the ability of partners to ease each other's fears. It seems that the better we are at easing each other's fears and doubts, the better we are at handling our relationship problems, and the more willing our partners are to commit to us. Some of us are happy having fleeting relationships, having someone to share a warm bed and a lustful embrace for a few short moments. The rest of us would rather have something more meaningful—a relationship that is deeper, a "happily ever after" romance with someone we can grow old with.

We all want to believe that fairy tale romances do exist. But we tend to omit the gritty, the struggles, and how much effort is needed to keep a relationship robust. Too many of us want the wedding, but not the marriage.

Happily ever after doesn't mean we won't struggle or argue, or that there will be no hurting from time to time. It isn't really "happily ever after;" it's more a case of "after we overcome our struggles, we'll be happy again". Rather than expecting things to be smooth sailing and problem free, it's better to be realistic. Life is full of challenges. This much is certain. It's how we deal with the uncertainties of the future; how we overcome our fears and challenges that determine whether a romance is "happily ever after" or not.

The answer is security or stability, being able to give each other the confidence to keep going while acting as each other's rock or safe haven. The future is uncertain, but with our loved ones giving us stability or security in the knowledge that they're there for us, it doesn't feel as daunting. We can find happiness as we, working together, overcome the issues that constantly bombard us.

We're all riddled with fear. It's normal. It's an inescapable part of being human. The reason fear and love go hand in hand is because they're an inseparable set of emotions. The more we love someone, the more we care and want to protect him/her. As a result, we become so attached, that it makes us fearful when something threatens our bond. The more someone becomes our source of joy, the more protective we become and the more fearful they be taken from us.

When we decide we want a real commitment with our partners, we can begin to worry. We are concerned because we aren't sure they feel the same way about us. We stress that they may not want to be with us over the long haul, even as we become more attached to them. If they don't feel the same way, the hurt escalates over time, especially since we get more attached to them with each passing day.

Our fear is that after having spent so much time sharing ourselves, opening our hearts to them, and putting all our efforts into loving them, one day they may simply disappear. They could go "poof," taking our heart with them.

Many of us can get so fearful of being abandoned that it drives us to act in ways we would rather not. We may become more jealous, clingy, or needy because we're unsure whether they want to stay with us. Or, we may become cold and distant, unwilling to share any more of ourselves because we aren't sure they feel as intensely about us as we do about them. We watch for signs that they want to be with us as much as we want to be with them. Sometimes we wait for so long that we begin to feel disconnected. This is so often a fear we have but are unwilling to admit to ourselves, or to our partner.

And often, without realizing it, we are the ones instilling fear in them. We may actually be the ones who drive them to become clingy, needy, cold, distant, or controlling. Rather than easing their fears, we instead fuel them and become frustrated when they're smothering us with unexpressed insecurities.

How do we fan their fear of abandonment? Here are a few ways: our unwillingness to share, unwillingness to spend time, and unwillingness to make an effort to show them how much they mean to us. Maybe our actions and words are laced with uncaring feelings. We may be so driven to protect our sense of independence and freedom that we implicitly convey that we're quite able to disappear at any time, especially when there's trouble.

Partners harping about their need for freedom doesn't instill confidence in their relationship; playing aloof pushes people away. When we share and our partner withdraws or attacks us, it doesn't offer any sense of security.

No trust can be built if a partner points out our faults, how we constantly hurt them, are always nagging, are continuously complaining, because it makes us feel as if we aren't good enough for them. It makes us feel they'll only be with us until someone better comes along. We're their "current" choice not their "forever" choice.

Here's a little story. Perhaps you will be able to relate.

One day Angie (name changed to protect privacy) meets a person she's not really sure of, but decides to go on a date with her nonetheless. After some time, things develop and she begins to realize she likes him. They enjoy each other's company and begin to laugh at each other's jokes - even when they're not funny.

As the relationship blossoms they become attached to each other, and they start to spend more time together. Things are going so well that Angie starts to feel she can't envision a future without him. But as times pass she begins to look back, and she sees days turning into months, months turning into years—however the relationship seems stuck. There has been no progress toward sealing the deal.

Despite feeling loved and knowing he loves her, Angie begins to worry. She starts to question whether he really wants to be with her. It has been years since they first met and fell in love. Why hasn't marriage been mentioned yet?

Unsure of her intentions, and feeling as though she's getting older and needs to settle down and start a "happily ever after" with him, Angie drops hints here and there. She begins trying to figure out how he feels about her and what he wants from the relationship, but she's far too scared to actually say it out loud or ask him directly—fearful that, if she's too forward it might scare him away.

Does this story resonate with you? In this situation, we could be the ones who aren't ready, willing, or able to commit. Despite loving someone intensely and wanting to be with them indefinitely, we just don't want to jeopardize what we have right now. We don't want to destroy what we've worked so hard to build. Maybe it's our fear of commitment, having seen our parents or loved ones go through harsh breakups and divorces that instill doubt in us. We worry that marriage will only destroy our relationship.

Maybe it isn't that we're unwilling to commit. Maybe we haven't yet settled into our careers, or haven't saved up enough money to feel ready. Right now, it just doesn't seem right, we don't want to put our partners through hardship. We want to be able to care and provide for them. We want to know we can take care of our families before we take the plunge into marriage.

Or, maybe we still doubt the relationship. Despite our love, we want both of us to grow a little bit more, and want both to become more mature before we commit. Our partners may be struggling with their own personal issues, so we want to make sure we can be with them after they've worked through them.

Marriage seems like a massive leap of faith. We don't want to make the mistake of being with them, sharing our all, and giving ourselves away, only to have them leave us in the end. Why would anyone ever marry someone they're unsure of? We just want to spend a little bit more time so we can settle in with each other.

Whatever the reasons are, some of us feel we should be progressing and marriage seems like the next logical step in our relationships. Others may feel marriage will cause problems, or they simply aren't ready to take that next step. Why jeopardize something that seems to be going well with "marriage" when all it seems to do is make people take each other for granted?

When we're ready to take the next step, but our partners aren't, there can be a natural compulsion to push and, at times, demand for their love. We want to know they want to be with us. But the more we push, the less willing they are to give. We push, not realizing that we're reacting on our own fears and by demanding long term commitment we will only push them away.

But when we're the ones who need a little more time, we hold back. We can feel overwhelmed and frustrated by our loved ones pressing us to make a decision we haven't yet considered. When they pressure us, it increasingly makes us question the relationship. We have our own fears—why can't they see that? If only they could reassure us, tell us that nothing would change, that we would still love and support each other and that marriages don't ruin relationships — then maybe, just maybe, we'd be more willing to take the next step.

If this is how our relationships look, it's inevitable that we'll drive each other away. Rather than realizing that each of us is driven by different fears, we focus solely on our own needs. Everyone's fears are unique: for some of us, it's a need for security - to know that our loved ones want to be with us. For others, it's a need for freedom, to know that our loved ones will give us the space we need when we need it. At times, our loved ones will ask us to show our commitment by starting a family, moving in together, or getting married. These are all requests to give them a greater sense of security and to let them know our relationship is progressing and we aren't going to disappear, that we are as committed to the relationship as they are.

A very somber depiction of how many of us

live our lives is by looking at how a simple misunderstanding over what a partner wants versus what we want — can cause so many hardships and eventual breakups. It can be as simple as our partner wanting us to listen to them talk about a problem they have, and we feel the urge to go into the repair-it mode. We don't realize that in trying to fix it, in trying to offer solutions, everything is aggravated. And so we get frustrated. What our partner wants and what we think they need are not in sync, leaving both parties feeling unheard and hurt.

Whether it's a simple or complicated misunderstanding, we don't have to be constantly hurting each other, or persistently trying to get our needs met, or waiting until it's safe for us to give. Many of us are unwilling to risk being hurt, expecting our love ones to accept our lack of readiness, not realising our unwillingness to commit is what stoking their fears and hurts in the first place. We should learn to risk being hurt, bearing our heart, letting them know how precious they are too us.

Imagine a relationship where our partner is waiting for us to love them, waiting for us to let them know how much they mean to us. However, we so often refuse to comply because we're terrified of being hurt. How long do they have to wait for us to utter the simple words "I love you. You mean the world to me and so much more?" How long are we going to pretend we don't care as much as we really do?

Our loved ones crave security every bit as

much as we do. Being in an unsure relationship is utter hell for both parties, especially when, each and every day, we're falling deeper and deeper in love. It's very frustrating when we're giving our all, but we aren't sure if our partners have the same intentions.

No one wants to be in a long term relationship without direction, or fearing that if we utter the "L" word, "M" word, or any other word that points to commitment that everything around us will come crashing down. As we pick up the pieces, we're left heartbroken. We'd be slightly older, more bitter, and sadder than ever before, because it would seem everyone else has found love except us.

When this happens, some of us might feel our time is ticking away. As we mature, many of us can feel resentful, like we are being left on the shelf, while everyone else is pairing up. When life doesn't seem to go our way, many of us seem to accumulate greater emotional baggage. We may not intentionally express it, but an air of defeat and frustration can exude from us – whether we're a man or woman.

When we are in a rush to couple up, we may give out vibes of neediness, desperation, bitterness, or anger. Maybe it's these sorts of feelings that cause potential partners to pass us by. Some of us may feel we are in a rush to get married or have children, and come across as demanding, manipulating, or controlling as a result. We are all vulnerable to such feelings, especially when we don't feel seen.

Being with someone who is in a rush to get

married while we are still trying to sort ourselves out can be quite frustrating. Even though we may love them, enjoy their company, and want to be with them indefinitely, we may want to pace ourselves a bit more. We may also want to be with someone who doesn't have as many hang ups, and who is more willing to give us the time and space we need to sort out our lives.

When we're younger, we're so often driven to prove ourselves. Marriage becomes a thought only when our partner encourages and motivates us. As we're just starting out, we want to feel secure that our partner will be there during our struggle for success, and not just coming along for the ride. And if things happen to fall apart, we also want to feel secure that they will stay to help us pick up the broken pieces.

We're all human. We do things out of a need for security, out of desperation or fear. If we come across as controlling and demanding, it's because we're fearful our loved ones may leave us. Much of our show of strength is bravado, and an attempt to hide our weaknesses and fears. At times, out of desperation we set up unhealthy relationships, making our loved ones dependent on us. We end up using ultimatums and threats to get them to commit, or to make them stick around. These tactics may work in the short term, but a relationship like this is built on a weak foundation and likely to crumble. Then, what we feared most and tried to avoid, becomes the new reality.

Even with strong foundations, we want to feel secure in the relationship. And men and women seek that security in different ways. For example, although a man may feel it is too soon to make a long term commitment, he should understand that when a woman asks him to share and make an effort on special occasions, she is subconsciously asking him to put more energy and emotion into their overall relationship. Hopefully, over time, he may realize how much he wants to be with her and how much he loves her. So he should take the time, make the effort, and do things that please her. A man should realize that a woman may need him to do things he may not really understand, things he may think of as wasteful, but for a woman, they're symbolic of how he feels about her. When she sees her man doing things like spending time or money, she sees it as him conveying his willingness to be there for her — his unspoken agreement that he wants to have a life with her.

In relationships, we may have our own way of perceiving security and what commitment entails. Some people see commitment as a loss of freedom; others want it out of fear of abandonment. For many, marriage offers security; for others, commitment means death of freedom. We need to realize that security doesn't have to come at the cost of our independence. If anything, freedom is found in security. The freedom to pursue our dreams and what brings us happiness comes with the security of knowing that someone loves us and wants to be there with us and for us.

*"Let them know your intentions –
we all like to have some certainty
about the destination."*

Chapter 11

Love is a Choice, Not an Obligation

We all have an ego and whether we like to admit it or not, it can be fragile. It may not take much for our egos to take a hit, causing us to feel sad or depressed. Reasons can include the constant buildup of life's stressors and demands which can push us to the brink. Tragedies like losing a job, a family member, or being told we have a serious illness, can take a toll on our psyche. No one, no matter how strong he or she is, is immune to the effects of life's tragedies and struggles. When we're stressed, pressured by work or besieged with lack of sleep having to care for a newborn, we can feel overwhelmed and isolated to a point in which our energy, confidence, and optimism are sapped.

Some people are able to recover quickly from stress and life's tragedies. Others do not bounce back as quickly as they'd like. Why is it that some people wrestle so much to recover from tragedy and stress while others seem to have such emotional strength? Despite life knocking them down, how is it they are able to stand back up, brush themselves off, and go about their lives as if nothing ever happened? It seems they've uncovered a secret that still bewilders the rest of us. Much of their resilience may be the by-product of having a support network of people who care for them when they're down, as well as having the necessary tools to go about getting the support they need when struggles present themselves. It's also partly because they have learned to accept themselves and understand that their mistakes are not failures, rather, they are attempts at understanding the world. As we grow and master life's challenges, we all stumble, fall, and struggle. Failures actually make us grow and become more mature.

Many people say that when we fall into life's struggles we should learn to get up, dust off, and try, try again. This is easier said than done. Sure, this sounds like an amazing concept, but in reality, it's not always as easy. Sometimes, the pain from the fall can leave us overwhelmed. Some of us are better at getting back up; others may need a little boost. Having to get back on our feet on our own takes a lot of courage, but it often takes more mettle to let others help us, to allow them to be our crutches, and see us at our lowest, most vulnerable points in life.

In these kinds of vulnerable times, we're all fragile. We don't need to pretend to be strong all the time. Sometimes our strength isn't even our own. It's a power we get from the support and encouragement of those who care for us. We gain strength from having a strong support system around us; we gain courage from allowing our loved ones in. We need to realize that part of what makes us strong are the relationships we build and foster around us. Strength isn't about suffering alone, but about suffering together, and helping each other with our challenges.

In times of struggle, it's easy to understand how important it is to receive love and to know what our loved ones think of us. The need to be grateful is obvious, although, to many of us, we can be overly lax in showing it. Assuming and expecting that our loved ones should already know we love them can sometimes cause us to fall into a pattern of taking each other for granted - a pattern of expecting them to accommodate our needs without voicing our appreciation. Many times, this kind of expectation can start to become an obligation we feel they must meet. We can start to feel it's our right, our privilege, and if they don't give love and support, we can see them as selfish. What we're forgetting is our loved ones give to us because they *want* to, not because they *have* to. Are they really being selfish for not wanting to give because they feel we're unappreciative? Isn't it far more selfish to expect them to give of themselves because we think loving us is an obligation that they should keep?

We expect their support and time, not realizing these things are actually gifts. Their willingness is very much subject to our ability to show them we appreciate their efforts. If we struggle with seeking support, we may also have trouble showing them how much we appreciate that backing. Not expressing our appreciation leaves others in doubt, so they hold back, unsure and worried about whether we'll notice their efforts the next time around.

We can expect everything to remain the same and that our partner will remain loving and devoted - that they will always be there for us. Satisfied with our initial efforts of appreciation, we may not notice our more recent lack of effort. Being too busy with life and its commitments, we can forget to take the time to show our partner that they matter to us. We can begin to forego simple pleasantries, like thanking them for a cooked meal, for how hard they work, or acknowledging their willingness to listen to our complaints and frustrations with empathy and understanding. We take for granted that it isn't our partner's duty to care for us; it's a gift that they offer to us on a daily basis. Love isn't just about grand gestures, it's also about the countless small contributions made every day. These are acts of unconditional love and caring, which inspire us to rush to our partner's arms every day, after a long day's work.

Many of us don't realize how fortunate we are to have someone precious in our lives. We realize how much they matter to us only after they have left, or have been taken by tragedy or sickness. More often than not, we only realize this after our partner has walked out for our lack of appreciation or acknowledgment, exhausted by the constant bickering, hurting, and fighting. In some cases, many of us have allowed our partner to walk away from us without realizing we actually played a role in making them leave by the way we treated them.

So, what can we do to make sure our partners love us enough and stay in the relationship? Make them feel fulfilled. Create a sense of belonging for them when they are with us. It isn't easy. It takes effort and commitment, but it is worth the healthy relationship that follows. Try to start by being grateful for each other and for the simplest things. Remember to say, "Thank you," and "You're welcome." These are powerful words that are not spoken enough in many relationships today. Work on saying daily to your partner, "Thank you for that all you do for me." When our loved ones hear this, it reassures them that you *are* in fact paying attention and you *are* grateful for them and for the things they do within the relationship.

The reason so many of us struggle in showing appreciation is because we believe showing love is something we should be doing in the shadows. Otherwise, it's just trying to gain attention or approval. But is there anything wrong with that? Is it so bad to want our partner and loved ones to notice our efforts? Is it so wrong to occasionally feel a little needy, or unsure, and to be reminded that they want to be with us? This is a flawed myth that needs to be busted.

Too many of us expect our partner to notice our efforts, wanting them to acknowledge our contributions, and yet at the same time believe that love is something to express only as seldom as it's required to spark romance. But when loved ones don't recognize our efforts, we become frustrated and annoyed, thinking they're ungrateful, unappreciative, or that they don't care about us. We get annoyed with them for not noticing us, but at the same time, we aren't willing to ask for their attention. It's likely we're afraid of being honest about our fears, worried that our occasional neediness might scare them away.

If our partner doesn't notice our efforts, is it really because they don't care about us? Are they really being ungrateful? Maybe they don't notice because they have other things on their mind. Maybe they're distracted by work and other commitments. How can we expect them to be thankful for something they don't notice in the first place?

Sometimes, we need to be reminded about how much our partner contributes to us. Sometimes, we need them to point out how and why they're doing something to provide for us. It isn't that we don't care, it's because we don't recognize it.

Don't be ashamed for seeking recognition for your efforts. It's okay to want to know you aren't being taken for granted. Thinking they should be appreciated for something they don't see will only cause unnecessary hurt. Many of us think that asking our loved ones to notice our efforts is an act of selfishness. But isn't pussyfooting, constant passive-aggressive silence, withdrawing, or withholding our love and constantly nagging also a form of selfishness in disguise? Either way, we're trying to get our loved ones to notice us, to notice our contributions and we're saddened when they don't. It's our unwillingness to be honest about our feelings, when we are taken for granted and neglected, that leads to damaging forms of manipulation and control, like nagging, criticism or wallowing in hurt in ways that make it impossible for them to ignore. Instead of sharing our vulnerabilities, we show frustration and anger, and then wonder why our loved ones become defensive.

As children, we are taught to give for the others' sake. We are taught that we need to be humble about our good deeds. Many of us learn not to flaunt how we contribute to the happiness of others, not to share how we're trying to make a difference to the world and those around us, that it is not right to seek recognition, or to have our efforts acknowledged because to want this sort of credit is a sign of selfishness. But the belief that we should be humble when contributing to the happiness of loved ones is flawed. It doesn't stack up. How can they appreciate us? How can we appreciate them? To appreciate something, we first need to notice it. Humility has its place, but not at the cost of each other's well-being. For loved ones to appreciate something, we first need to let them know that what we're doing is for *their* benefit.

Take the time to slow down, breathe, and look around. There are plenty of reasons to be appreciative. Many reasons are taken for granted, and happen when we're absent, so they go unnoticed. We all do little things to show love on daily basis: washing the dishes, making the bed, refueling the car, paying the bills, or preparing dinner. Whatever it may be, we do so many little things every day to show how we care for each other. Many of these things are done out of sight. So, we should take the time to show appreciation, and to let our partners know that their efforts don't go unnoticed. Relationships thrive on daily gestures of care and appreciation that help foster giving.

"It is their choice to love us,

not an obligation."

Chapter 12

Not Always What They Want

We all like to think of ourselves as considerate beings who care for our loved ones, but what does it really mean to be considerate? The general idea is to always be mindful of the welfare of others. As much as we try, others will still occasionally think we are being inconsiderate. Overall, we are thoughtful, but when hurts are triggered, consideration is often forgotten or ignored. We sometimes will even go as far as hurting others to limit our own hurt.

Being considerate is being thoughtful of how actions affect others, but we all still struggle at times. Despite knowing what thoughtfulness is, it isn't always easy to know how others will interpret our actions. It isn't always easy to know how we affect loved ones. When we share and express ourselves, our loved ones may not understand our words or see our gestures in the same light. Despite our efforts to care for them, they may not see things the same way. At times, they may even see us as uncaring and failing to take into account how they feel.

Being insensitive isn't necessarily an intention to hurt others. It is the lack of understanding that others may interpret our actions and words as being hurtful. We are considered indifferent when we're unwilling to consider how the feelings of others may differ from our own. It's an expectation that their feelings should always be in sync with our own that causes so much heartache.

Often, when I was growing up, the people close to me labeled me as "mean" or "insensitive." At first, I wasn't sure what they meant. It wasn't that I intended to hurt them. It wasn't that I was being argumentative; I was simply being defensive.

My tendency to be self-protective goes back to when I was younger. I grew up emotionally numb so I can cope with my pain, and I thought that was just how everyone should deal with their emotions. As a result, I became deaf and blind to the hurting of others. In addition to the numbness, I dealt with my hurts and frustration by making light of them, laughing them off. I belittled the situation so it wouldn't sting as much. But the problem was I expected others to do the same. How wrong and insensitive I was – not because I was trying to be, but because I didn't realize they were dealing with their hurt in their own unique way.

Being seen as insensitive can sometimes boil down to a matter of personal style. I have a forthright personality, and I tend to put comments out there in a matter-of-fact way. I've had to learn the subtleties of how to speak, including the nuances in voice tone, choosing the right words, how to string sentences together, and even the art of pausing and slowing down.

Given my personality, the history of my hurts and coping mechanisms I developed to deal with emotional wounds, I've had to make a systematic effort to learn how not to come across as insensitive, and learn to be much more expressive about my feelings. Just like me, many people can be unaware of how their words and actions can injure others. They can also be unwilling to admit this. It takes a lot of effort to realize the effect that we have on others, to realize that they might be justified in accusing us of being insensitive.

At times, our attempts at encouragement and support may come across as condescending, critical, or careless. When this happens, take a step back. Consider that your words and intentions aren't always in sync, and that your words and actions won't always be seen as helpful. In the past, I found that the main reason others saw me as inconsiderate was because my choice of words and tone of voice conveyed insensitivity. And, my words and tone sometimes reflected that I was distracted, which made others feel I wasn't being present with them. I can see now how my poor choice of words caused my loved ones' hurt and frustration. The reason they regarded me as indifferent boiled down to my need to protect myself. When I became aware that my words and the way I portrayed myself were at the root of their frustration, I became more open and honest with myself—and with others.

Simply sharing my thoughts with others and owning up to my own hurt and irritation eased my need to protect myself. I no longer needed to be defensive because I could see their annoyance was due to their doubts and hurt feelings. Rather than rejecting what they were experiencing, or arguing that their feelings weren't justified, I looked into how my words accidentally hurt. More often than not, my loved ones merely needed reassurance, to ease their own fears and doubts. I unintentionally caused them hurt and, the more I fought back and rejected the idea that my words came across as harsh, more pain and frustration surfaced.

No one is born adept with words. As one who struggled with the English language throughout my childhood and much of my early adulthood, I understand how difficult it can be. Being eloquent, knowing what to say, or how to phrase things in a way that won't injure or offend others, didn't always come easy for me. Much of it was learned through trial and error. What made it easier was my willingness to take responsibility for how I expressed myself. There seems to be a tacit link between how ready we are to accept the role our words can play in affecting others, and how good we are at getting our needs heard and met. Comforting others helps us get our own needs met.

Clear, effective, and compassionate communication is a skill that requires careful practice and refining. Since I knew how difficult it was, how I fumbled and stumbled with my words, I came to realize how problematic it can be for others. Recognizing that they would occasionally blunder with their words, rather than finding myself blindsided, I somewhat expected others to say hurtful things, not because they were trying to harm me, but because they didn't know how to express themselves elegantly. Giving others the benefit of the doubt made them much more willing to listen to my own words. This allowed me to express myself and to see that my feelings of hurt were warranted. I knew they may very well damage me, but I also knew it was not their intent. So I learned to focus on their intent, not on how they delivered a message. Taking this approach helped me deal with the needs of others. It no longer felt like a competition, and they no longer saw me as blaming them. It made people more receptive, more elegant, and more careful with their words.

By focusing on intent, instead of fixating on content, I saw how others often struggled with how they were trying to express themselves. I gave them the benefit of the doubt and allowed them to mess-up with words. Discovering this was exactly what I needed when I started out on my personal development path. It dawned on me that they also needed the same consideration!

Understanding how people can be insensitive has allowed me to find ways to be more sympathetic. What I've found is that being considerate is getting over ourselves, and realizing and accepting we may not always be understood. It's the realization that misunderstandings are real things. Despite how much effort we put into trying to be clear at times, we still need to explain and clarify what we really mean. By accepting misinterpretation as a normal part of life, I started to get more in tune with the feelings of others. Accepting that misunderstanding will forever be a possibility in human communication helped me stop reacting inappropriately to others. Curbing the inclination to become defensive and guarded made me more daring to ask questions. No longer shielded, I began delving a little deeper and making a little more effort. I came to see others for who they are and not for what I previously thought them to be: they're merely people with jumbled up fears and insecurities, just like me.

Over the years, through a lot of trial and error, I also came to realize there are two possible ways to show consideration for one another. The first is by approaching "giving" as an act of self-sacrifice. In other words, we shelve our own needs to take care of the needs of others. The second approach is when we free others from the burden of caring for us; we ease their need to care for us by hiding our distress and/or refusing to ask too much of them.

It's a simple distinction, but was a profound revelation. It shows how we manifest consideration in different ways, sometimes in methods that our partners don't recognize.

> *"I will satisfy you, you will satisfy me, and we will satisfy each other.*
>
> *I will satisfy myself, you will satisfy yourself, and we will satisfy ourselves."*

This simple distinction can mean the difference between feeling cared for and feeling overwhelmed by the needs of others. Some people approach the act of giving by looking for ways to please, or bring happiness, to a loved one. Others approach consideration by looking for ways to shoulder some of their loved ones' burdens or reduce their stress.

Concern could be expressed by taking a greater burden upon ourselves to care for our partners, and expecting them to do the same for us. But consideration can also include wanting to take care of ourselves, ensuring that our partners won't need to worry about us, thus giving them greater freedom. When we choose the latter, we expect our partners to temporarily reduce their expectations of us. An example of this would be when we ask others not to intrude into our personal space unless invited. One approach focuses on giving pleasure, the other on taking away pain. Either way, these are attempts to be considerate. When it comes down to it, we all want our loved ones to be thoughtful. Being considerate requires us to learn to accommodate what it means to our partners.

When I stopped defending myself and started asking questions, I learned that others' ideas about being "inconsiderate" or "insensitive" stemmed from not believing their feelings mattered to me. They were unsure about how much I really cared for them. By starting to approach my relationships with the intention of finding ways to be more considerate, I've learned what it truly means, and I in turn sowed the seeds to my own fulfillment in the process.

Chapter 13

Struggling to Share

We all strive for happiness and a better tomorrow; even though much of it is for our own sake, it's also for the benefit of the ones we love. In fact, our accomplishments are always meant to be shared with those most precious to us. Overcoming life's challenges is draining enough, and at times, we can feel down as though nothing seems to fit. Strive as we may, our confidence gets squashed by life's constant demands and all of the responsibilities that come with them.

When we're drained and exhausted, we turn to our partners in the hope of finding strength. We search to find reassurance, to be reminded of our capabilities, because we aren't sure whether tomorrow will bring a better day. We turn to those we love for their confidence in us because it's in their eyes we find our own happiness.

This is why simple words of encouragement and reassurance can make a huge difference. But despite being aware of this, a lot of times we can struggle to say things like: "I believe in you." "I trust you can do it." "Even if things don't go our way, as long as we are together, we can piece it together and start anew." Everyone needs to hear reassuring, encouraging words from time to time. This is because sometimes courage can't be found inside us. Sometimes strength has to be borrowed from those who support us, like a friend, a partner, or even a stranger.

Feeling supported makes us want to try a little harder, to dare to leave our comfort zone and work more diligently than we would otherwise. Words are powerful; they can be made into instruments of mayhem—which can leave others emotionally distraught—or tools of empowerment, easing worries and giving others strength they didn't know they had.

In moments of doubt and worry, we can need a reason to try harder. It can be a simple reminder of why we slave away at work and that may be so we can care for those we love and depend on us. Even though we may know why we strive for more, at times doubts and worries fester. For me, as someone who wants to constantly stretch and push himself, at times I've felt very alone as I strive for a slice of a better life and fight for a better world. A few times I've even felt trapped in a spiral of depression and frustration, unable to claw my way out.

It's during times when our zest for life has chipped away, and our hardened shell of resilience and confidence has cracked, that we need words of encouragement. Drained and doubtful, we become far more vulnerable than usual, needing a stable, nurturing environment to turn to. We need an emotional safe haven where we can recharge.

We all cry out for recognition and encouragement—perhaps not explicitly, but we do. It may become evident between the lines we speak. It might be teary eyes from a sleepless night spent tossing and turning. Maybe it's expressed through our frustration or annoyance at trivial things.

Or, perhaps, it is not expressed at all. All too often the suffering happens in silence. Before, I would numb my pain in that silence. Not wanting to appear needy or desperate kept me silent. When I look at others, so often I can see the suffering in their eyes and on their faces. I can hear it in their words. So much of what they say resonates with me, all because I have been in their shoes. Many of us have been there or we know someone who has suffered in isolation because they were too afraid of making themselves vulnerable to another person.

The last thing we want for our loved ones is for them to suffer in silence, to feel isolated, or to believe they have to deal with everything on their own. This is the last thing anyone wants to feel: that whatever they're going through doesn't matter. By observing dysfunctional relationships around me, including my own, I found a more effective way to approach these situations. I watched people who were eloquent with their words and could point out others' wrongdoing without leaving them feeling unhappy or picked to pieces. It may sound strange, but with "critics" like these, you'd feel blessed to be criticized. You'd feel driven rather than defeated. As I read about miraculous people who could do this, people like Dale Carnegie, Bill Gates, and Warren Buffett, I wondered how some people can be so powerful that, even while criticizing, they're still able to elevate a person. While others, even when praising can leave others feeling defeated and belittled. At times, the message is the same, but the way it's relayed differs greatly.

Why are some people more effective than others? By watching and listening to them, I realized it all comes down to how well we're able to communicate hurt and frustration without belittling others in the process. People who communicate well can share themselves without making others feel threatened and share their feelings without instilling the fear of being rejected, criticized, or judged.

Everyone wants to share themselves, but many struggle with being able to express themselves elegantly. I had a problem with this for many years. My tendency to get annoyed made others recoil. So, whenever I wanted to share, my loved ones weren't willing to listen. When I expressed myself, what I revealed seemed more like criticism to them. They became defensive for reasons I didn't understand. It was frustrating being in a relationship where I felt unable to share. Banging my head against the wall, I tried to find the secret formula to instilling in others a willingness to express their feelings while at the same time making sure they were still willing to listen to mine.

I succeeded when I realized I have as much power over them as they have over me. We all hold more power than we realize. The struggles and problems we face in life are mostly of our own doing. Our loved ones' defensiveness is a reflection of ourselves, but when we start sharing and owning the hurt (admitting our fears and insecurities) those around us will begin to be less guarded. It isn't always *what* we say that matters; it's *how* we say it. Many of us become defensive and argue because we feel attacked, but at the same time, we trigger defensiveness in others because of the way we express our feelings to them.

A whole new world opened up to me when I began working on how I phrased things. Learning to express ideas and thoughts in ways that didn't make others feel threatened, made them less prone to defensiveness. Others became more welcoming of my opinions and feelings.

We enter into relationships to share our pains and worries and to overcome the challenges of life together. Sharing helps ease pain; we don't have to carry the load on our own. We don't need to suffer in isolation. We all want to give ourselves openly and honestly. We all want support and encouragement when we need it.

Over the years, everyone develops ways of dealing with their pain. Some people can rely on others to ask probing questions and pick up nuances in their words and tone, expecting others to know what to say or do to make them feel better. Others withdraw into themselves. Trying to detach from their emotions, they become numb to the outside world. Others turn to drugs, alcohol or other destructive habits in an attempt to escape the rampant pain that lies inside. Exhausted and drained, they wrap themselves in cocoons that make them seem uncaring or emotionally absent.

It isn't that we're unwilling to share; it's that we need to recover within ourselves *before* we can share. We need to build back up emotional strength and self-confidence before we feel able to share. But it's this need to recover before sharing that makes our loved ones feel as though we don't care about them. They may just be in need of a sympathetic ear, but when they turn to us, we appear withdrawn and closed off. We're supposed to be there for them, but the more they push us to listen, the more withdrawn we become.

There are plenty of reasons why some of us have a need to share, while others prefer to disconnect. For me, the reason I withdrew was I feared losing control, or accidentally saying something insensitive that might increase a loved one's frustrations, leading him/her to criticize and attack me. I withdrew to avoid getting hurt. I was trying to avoid confrontation, not realizing I was also giving people the impression that their feelings didn't matter to me.

Whenever I was emotionally drained and others wanted to support me, it felt as if they were pushing and prodding. Because I was hurting, it all too often felt intrusive. Rather than making me share, it made me push away more. I saw them as demanding because they didn't allow me to share at my own pace. But one time, when I looked into my partner's teary eyes, it dawned on me that loving another person wasn't easy. I realized her pushing and prodding was her attempt to try to understand my feelings, her attempt to try and find out how much she mattered to me, while at the same time trying to keep her own guard up. Fearful and worried that her feelings may not be reciprocated, she prodded and pushed, pushed and prodded, hoping I would make the first move.

The one first willing to confess "I love you" will bear the brunt of being hurt. No one wants to be first to endure the possibility of being rejected. We prod and push, hoping to pick up little hints in the tone, words, and actions of our loved ones, trying to understand where we stand in their future plans.

Those who like to share will want others to do the same, and they will find it frustrating when their partners withdraw into themselves. We assume the ways we deal with our distress should also work for others; after all, our loved ones should be like us, right? Some feel it's the only way to get our loved ones to listen to us. We expect them to be receptive, but we don't realize the act of pushing and prodding is what makes them withdraw or become defensive. As we focus on trying to get them to listen, and having our needs met, we forget to remind them that it's safe to share; we forget the crucial step of reassuring them they're not being attacked. We jump straight to getting our needs met while forgetting that no one is willing to share (or listen) unless they feel it's safe to do so.

And when they do share, sometimes what our partners want is the opposite of what they say. We can all send out mixed signals. Our loved ones may seem to be pushing us away but, in truth, they're actually testing us to see how much we're willing to stand by them. Their cold, nonchalant acts are attempts to hide how fearful they are. It's mostly the fear of becoming exposed to another person. This is why taking a step of vulnerability and sharing is so crucial to the health of a relationship. We all want the same thing: to know it's safe to share ourselves.

Our loved ones want to know whether we want to be with them as much as they want to be with us. Most of our worries may not be openly or explicitly expressed, but from time to time, these fears crop up, urging us to take drastic action to soothe them. We may try to test our partner's conviction, to check their willingness to love us, despite being less than our lovable selves. Juggling these two fears—wanting to know we're not in a one-sided relationship while being fearful of getting hurt or becoming vulnerable to another person—makes it difficult to freely express ourselves. Dropping hints and clues, probing for answers or responses can be like playing a game of charades. We all do it, in one way or another - trying to get our needs met without making ourselves susceptible. Even the act of playing mind games, pushing and pulling, is an attempt at avoiding becoming vulnerable with a loved one.

When we struggle to share, there are many reasons why knowing the right things to do and say isn't always easy. Mixed signals are constantly being sent out; hidden clues are being dropped here and there. Sifting through what our loved one's real feelings are and separating them from their actions can be difficult. Like a waiting trap, one wrong assumption can blow up in our faces. But despite the difficulties, one thing we can be sure of is that we all want our loved ones to stand by their conviction to love us. And the process of loving means it's all right to be vulnerable; it's okay to not always be strong. It means we are letting our loved ones know they can lean on us because *we* want them to.

"When they feel heard, supported and encouraged,

*they are **better partner**s, **lover**s**, parent**s, and **friend**s."*

Chapter 14

It's Quality over Quantity of Time

We all have plenty on our plate to keep us busy, whether it is a demanding job or looking after our budding young family. Whatever it is, by the end of the day we can feel emotionally and physically spent that we barely have enough energy for ourselves, let alone catering to the needs of loved ones. But by giving everything else attention, we can begin to neglect our relationships, expecting them to remain as they are without realizing that a chasm is opening between us and our loved ones. We're so busy that we wonder why passion dwindles, why our partners seem so distant... so different.

It takes effort to keep the proper chemistry in balance. Relationships aren't always easy. When times are tough, we may feel like giving up. However, like anything that's worth caring about, it's worth spending time to become better at restoring the chemistry that brought us together and kept us close with our loved ones. Putting in effort to spend quality time with them rekindles the connection. It's a gentle reminder that we are part of each other's worlds. The amount of time it takes to feel and remain connected to each other differs from person to person, and to some, it may seem daunting, but a lack of effort will definitely force a wedge between loved ones. The longer we go on neglecting our loved ones, and avoid getting involved in their lives, the more we grow apart. Sooner or later we become estranged; our relationships will feel more like a communion between strangers than a relationship between lovers. We may still love each other—very much so—but we just don't know each other anymore. We don't love our partners the same way we did because we feel that person we fell in love with, is no longer there. They seem so different because they have grown over time. Who they are at the core is still there, but because they may have gone through many challenges and learned some life lessons, they can feel like a different person. Just like them, we may have grown and changed too. Not feeling connected can also be a combination of both partners growing and changing. We may feel like we no longer understand each other. By not spending enough quality time, we can end up feeling like our partners have changed. They are not the same person we fell in love with several years ago.

To stay connected, it's crucial to take time out for each other. Many times it isn't easy putting our needs aside, or the workload that's piling up, but we must make an effort to make time for each other. Isn't our foremost responsibility towards our partner's well-being? Isn't it our responsibility to ensure that our loved ones have enough courage, confidence, and conviction to pursue their heart's desires? Part of the reason why we get into relationships in the first place is to have someone to share moments of triumph and doubt.

In my youth, I naively thought it was about spending as much time together as possible, and having my world revolve around those I loved. Every dream, every goal, must somehow have them in the picture, and if it didn't I felt somewhat guilty for neglecting or abandoning them. It was a mix of emotions, though. Sometimes I felt it was a chore to spend time with them - something I had to do out of obligation. I dedicated many hours to them, but I was never truly present, constantly withdrawn and distracted by other things. My partners could sense I really didn't want to be there and, at the end I would seem somewhat bitter, frustrated, and emotionally tired.

When I switched from spending a lot of time with my partners to focusing more on the quality of time I spent with them, my love relationships greatly improved. So did the relationship with my family. Taking care of their well-being doesn't have to take long. It's about spending the time earnestly and honestly, consoling them in their moments of doubt and fear, cheering and sharing their enthusiasm for all their achievements. When I decided to be truly present with them, they were able to be much more present with me.

We're all human, subject to human feelings, fears, and mistakes, and sometimes we stumble. When our loved ones do, they want us to take the time to ease their doubting minds and let them know they are cared for. Anyone who feels daunted by the responsibilities of life wants to know they have someone in their corner, someone to share their pain, someone who understands them and is willing to stand beside them, not just when the weather is fair, but even when it's foul; they need someone who will be by their side during the good times and the bad. We want our loved ones to be more than just ships passing in the night; we want them residing permanently by our side. It's comforting to know someone wants to be with us and wants to entwine their roots with ours.

To reach that kind of closeness, we need to know the difference between spending time and spending "quality" time with our loved ones. Sitting in front of the television together watching the news doesn't count. Neither does spending time listening to the other person while distracted by other things like work or our own worries. Quality time is spent in earnest communion trying to understand, care, support, and be present for our loved ones as they share themselves and their concerns with us. Quality time offers the opportunity to bond, to feel reassured by each other's presence, and to remind each other we're there in the midst of our struggles. Spending quality time allows both parties to share the new, rediscover the old, and appreciate the growth that has taken place individually and together. It allows us to be a pleasure in each other's lives, rather than feeling like a chore or an obligation. When we're spending quality time, both parties simply become much more pleasant to be around.

How do we start to spend quality time? A simple first step is to allocate a block of time, say an hour or a few hours a week, where you spend time with your loved ones on an individual basis. Do things they want to do and that they enjoy. During this time, focus on them - ask them about things that have happened in their lives, their challenges and aspirations. Let them feel you care and are at their service. The more we can do this, the more the quality of our relationships will improve.

"Quality time is key to feeling close and connected."

Chapter 15

Tokens to Remember

A hug or kiss is something that's hard to share when thousands of miles separate us from our loved ones. Sometimes what's needed is something to compensate for our absence, something tangible to hold, touch, smell or see - something that reminds them we're thinking about them. The gift doesn't need to be grand. At times the simplest things suffice, such as a t-shirt sprayed with our partner's fragrance, a special memento, or love letters. Long distance relationships can be difficult to maintain, but as long as our loved ones can see the effort, love, and tenderness behind our gestures, our attempts at reminding them how often we're thinking of them will be genuinely accepted and appreciated. It isn't the price tag that matters; it's the thought that goes into it.

Whenever a gift is given, the receiver can often think to themselves: "How much thought and effort went into this?" A thoughtless gift can have the opposite effect to the intended purpose, like giving steak knives to a vegetarian or a bottle of vodka to a recovering alcoholic. It isn't about giving gifts; the gifts themselves should reflect the recipients' individual preferences. Showing the recipient we thought about them — their real selves, their likes and dislikes, — make the act of carefully picking out the gift even more important than the present itself. It shows our partner that we *do* know them, that we are paying attention to their thoughts, stories, opinions, quirks, likes, and dislikes. It shows them we care enough to take the time to understand their needs and wants.

Simple, safe gifts are a good start. A dozen roses does wonders when our partners seem down, and a box of chocolates will skyrocket when they're not just given on St. Valentine's Day. Tickets to a loved one's favorite kind of entertainment event, or favorite band can also be great ideas. So can mementos, because of what they symbolize. It's the effort and thought that goes into them that gives them so much meaning.

When we are the recipient, the fact that our loved ones have gone out of their way to show us their affection makes us feel loved and understood. Actions like these ease our fears and doubts. They reflect the concern for our well-being, giving attention to our needs and a willingness to care for us.

Getting the "wrong" gift can help us understand how poorly-selected gifts can cause loved ones to feel the same way. It can feel frustrating if the gift doesn't cater to our individuality. "Wrong" gifts reflect our lack of understanding or effort, as well as our inability to care for them in the ways they need. But when we receive them, we need to realize that the mere giving of the gift is better than withholding affection. The act itself conveys they're trying to love and better understand us. They may get it wrong - we didn't really want that itchy blue sweater with the face of Santa Claus printed on it. It may have been so embarrassingly ugly we wouldn't even force our own dog to wear it - but we need to realize that gifts come from the heart. They're giving a piece of themselves to us – it's just that they have poor taste in clothing. This is why we should be more appreciative of all the little gifts we receive, even when they miss the mark. It's better to just let others know what it is we prefer next time. Being unappreciative and showing disappointment by what we receive will only make them less willing to give. It's better to appreciate what we receive and clearly communicate what it is we want, as this will improve our chances of getting what we want next time.

This is a sensitive topic for many people. Learning to give what another person wants isn't easy, especially when there's a growing expectation that partners should already know each other well enough so that neither should have to voice their needs. A simple exchange of gifts is always laced with emotions, frequently of fondness. When our partners give us a gift, it's supposed to reflect their fondness for us. But when we show disappointment in their efforts, they can feel like we are rejecting them.

Greater care should be taken when we show appreciation for gifts. It helps give others confidence and a willingness to explore new ways of giving and going forward. Being grateful for everything gives us all the courage and confidence to be ourselves, to share with each other more honestly and more earnestly. It lays a strong foundation so that giving to each other becomes the norm.

Since it isn't always easy to know what to give someone, here's a simple exercise to help you. Make a list of little things you can randomly give to your special someone every day for the next three weeks. Get in tune with the other's needs and wants. Listen to him/her; study him/her. Think of all the special items that will put a smile on his/her face. Here's a start:

For guys giving to gals:

- A single rose
- A bar of chocolate
- A handwritten card
- Shopping for groceries so she does not have to
- A framed picture of the two of you
- Popping by her office and dropping off lunch for her
- A copy of this book

For gals giving to guys:

- Tickets to a favorite sporting event
- A magazine on one of his hobbies – e.g., *Car, Men's Health*
- A discreet sexy picture of you
- One of his favorite computer games

- A tool or gadget he had his eyes on
- A copy of this book

"Keep them giving by showing enthusiasm and appreciation for the little gifts they give."

Chapter 16

Yearning for a Connection

My journey of learning the lessons of connection and vulnerability did not come easily. The first girl I allowed myself to be open with and to bear my all with, broke my heart and left me devastated. After that, I closed up. In time, I took the risk again. My ex-fiancée, she was the second woman I ever opened up to. Throughout our relationship, I had a massive fear of commitment, a fear of getting close and being hurt. Sharing and letting her in felt scary. Before her, my relationships had been numbing experiences. I pretended I was a player, thinking I could get any girl, but that was far from the truth. I just wasn't willing to be vulnerable or commit to another person because I was too scared of falling in love.

At the time, I was quite amateurish in relationships; I didn't know what to do or how to share myself. Taking a relationship seriously was new to me. There were times when frustrations reached a boiling point and we unintentionally took it out on each other, pushing each other away, oftentimes blaming each other for our suffering. There were times when we got upset, and wrongly blurted out that we hurt statements even though deep down we knew that was not true. You may resonate with how this can happen in relationships.

Deep down, when we love another person, we want them to stick around, fight for our love, and stand by us even in times where they're finding it difficult to love us.

Like myself, many of us act tough, pretending that nothing fazes us and we can handle things on our own, but this portrayal is seldom true. We may well be better able to deal with challenges alone, but that doesn't mean we want to. We may be able to cope with life's challenges better on our own at times, but the thought is just bravado, an attempt to protect our soft inner core. We act tough to fool ourselves, hoping that we will start to believe the facade we project – and at times we do.

Behind the façade lies our vulnerabilities. Facing them is hard enough, but it can be even harder to show them if we're unsure if our partners will respond with affection. It's hard to ask someone to love us when we're in our weakest, most feeble, and vulnerable states. No matter who we are, no matter how strong we may seem, this is one of the hardest things to do. It works the other way, too; it's frustrating trying to love our partners when they are feeling vulnerable, rather than share their hurt with us, they instead attack us. In those moments, we need to be able to see past their bravado to the underlying hurt.

When our loved ones are angry with us — telling us to go away— we can leave, taking their words literally; or we can slow down, let our frustrations subside, and listen. Their quivering voice and tearful eyes say it all, but they may hold back because they don't want us to see their hurt.

We may very well understand this feeling, having felt that way ourselves. They're scared of rejection, of being hurt more than they already are, so they may not be willing to admit that they really want us to stay, even if "staying" just means staying on the other side of a door.

At times like these, it's about letting them know we're within reach, that we are there for them. It relieves loved ones when they know we want to be in their lives, we're willing to support them and stand beside them during difficult times. Through the gift of presence, we can be there to care for them and be their safety net when things are bad.

It's hard enough trying to be each other's support; it's even harder when loved ones push us away. Not because they don't care about or love us, but because they're dealing with their own challenges or painful experiences. Pushing us away can hurt, and lead to blaming them for our pain. Being on the receiving end of the blame - the cause of their upset state - is a terrible feeling. Since we know how it feels, why would we want to put our loved ones through this kind of torture?

To truly connect and reach mutual understanding, we need to learn to let down our walls and be there for each other. When our relationships are built on giving and learning to be of better service to each other, the urge to withdraw, blame, or criticize wanes. We won't need to build fronts of strength because we'll feel sufficiently secure in the relationship. We'll feel we can express our fears and worries openly and honestly, knowing that whatever happens, we will be there for each other no matter what.

*"Our presence gives them comfort
that when we're needed,
we're easily within reach."*

Chapter 17

Love is the Art of Showing Affection

Feeling the tender, intimate touch of a loved one reminds us we're not alone in the world. It instills the sense that we're cared for and that someone wants to share moments of sadness—not just joys—with us. A tender touch or sweet thoughtful words can mean the difference between life and death, especially when we're struggling. At times, we simply can't reach out to our loved ones for the support we need, but their tokens of affection are much appreciated. Sadly though, many of us struggle and suffer in silence and let (or expect) our loved ones do the same.

It's sad when people stand by and watch their loved ones spiral into depression. Affection and tenderness are what we all seek in relationships. They're the cure for the suffering we go through from time to time. Loneliness and isolation are very real things. It's scary to think our loved ones may find themselves in such a state, but they do. Pretending it won't happen, or that our love ones are impervious to it, isn't going to make them immune. At times, affection is what keeps us going, fighting against the pull of depression, enduring the hardships of life. It instills in us the notion of hope that tomorrow will be a better day — and most of the time, it's true.

The precious moments of being connected can make a person wonder why some people opt to stay single. The connection we feel, while we're in our loved ones' embrace, make us feel that life's problems and challenges are not as daunting as it seem. When we're with each other, nothing seems to matter beyond that wonderful, selfless moment, just feeling and appreciating each other, enjoying each other's presence and love. Despite the uncertainties of life and the future, we know that we have someone to face them with, hand-in-hand.

Humans thrive on intimacy. It's one of the major reasons why we seek relationships in the first place. It's sad that while we're distracted by life's tribulations we forget to show affection to our loved ones. We forget to do the little things that our partners want from us; the little things they appreciate so much.

Affection comes in many forms: a simple kiss on the forehead, stroking their hair while they're sitting next to you, or lying in each other's arms in silence. Affection is a simple, straightforward-enough idea, but often we let the chances to show warmth slip by. We assume we can do it later; our partners aren't going anywhere, are they? We're too busy at the moment and since there will be a lifetime of moments, we can show them affection at any time, right?

The problem with postponing affection is that it will undoubtedly lead others to feel neglected. What happens when your partner is struggling with pain, and needs your reassurance, but you let these moments pass you by because you were too busy?

And, each time you do, the warmth and connection between the two of you seems to dwindle. Eventually, s/he can feel as if you don't care anymore. The best time to show affection is right now. It only takes a fraction of a second — sometimes it's as simple as a genuine, sincere smile or an adoring look.

When it comes to showing affection, some people struggle. Particularly with some men, showing affection simply doesn't feel right. This can be because they never learned how to be affectionate. Perhaps in our attempts to be caring and supportive, we can come across as sarcastic, critical or judgmental. Showing affection may feel strange, so we feel somewhat stupid or fraudulent in the attempt. Many people misconstrue being affectionate with being romantic. Let's face it, not everyone is a Don Juan or Casanova. Some people couldn't prepare a romantic evening even if everything that's needed was all laid out in a box in front of them, instruction and all. Affection is different. Showing warmth and care is one of the simplest forms of expression. The problem is that many of us make it too complicated. Many people read way too much into what being affectionate actually means. Because it doesn't feel natural, we can think it's just not our style and give up attempting to show affection altogether.

At times, we're so concerned with how we look, with how our acts of affection will be received, that we don't bother trying in the first place. It's easier to act aloof than to be warm, caring, and affectionate. Many people mistakenly believe that those who are unwilling to show affection and warmth only do so because they don't care. This is simply not true. Many people struggle with showing warmth because they just don't know how. We're unsure of how to express our love, our concerns about the other, or what to do to make our partners feel better.

An inability to show affection is frequently because we, or our loved ones, fear the attempt will result in emotional pain. Because of the fear of hurt or rejection, we find it easier to show affection and tenderness to a child or pet. It feels safer. We know the child or pet will never reject us, or if they do, their rejection will be more bearable. We don't interject our insecurities into rejections like these. When it's someone we love, the potential for hurt is greater and more severe. For these reasons, many of us withhold tenderness. We aren't willing to put ourselves in what feels like an emotionally risky situation. Our coldness is a way to protect ourselves. The best way to avoid rejection is to reject first; this is what being cold, aloof and nonchalant is all about.

The truth is it's far easier to love children and pets than it is our partners. Greater expectations come from partners. Many of these expectations include knowing what we '"should" do, knowing how to give, knowing what they want. A child or pet is far more likely to reciprocate with affection even when we fail them in some way. Their needs and expectations are simpler; it's easier to understand what to do to satisfy them.

It seems strange, but at times, some people become jealous of pets or children because their partners give them far more attention and affection.

And our loved ones may even be more polite, considerate and thoughtful toward strangers than they are toward us, which can hurt. We become frustrated and feel somewhat silly or guilty for even feeling jealousy at times like these. For many of us, it seems inappropriate to be jealous of a child or stupid to think that our partners are more caring toward a pet than they are toward us—but is it?

Face it—at times our loved ones *are* more caring toward a pet cat than they are toward us, despite cats being known for their aloofness. Denying or avoiding our jealousy isn't going to change our feelings or the situation; in fact, it might cause additional harm to our relationships. There may be justified reasons to feel jealous, to feel we're competing with a pet or child for a partner's affection. Perhaps their inability to be tender with us makes us feel that they think we're undeserving or unworthy of their affection. We see they're fully capable of expressing tenderness, care and kindness—just not toward us.

Many people are guilty of showing affection toward everything and everyone except their partners. When we do this, we may not realize that our loved ones may very well feel neglected. Our inability to show them affection makes them feel as if they don't matter. When it happens to us, it hurts to think our loved ones care more for others than they do for us, or that their kindness is reserved for everyone else and all we seem to receive are their harsher leftovers. They seem willing to make efforts to be considerate to others, so why not us? This isn't something we like to think we're doing, but we do. At one point or another, we've all been guilty of showing our loved ones less kindness and affection than they deserve.

Make an effort to learn to be affectionate. It's a life skill like any other. Learning to be affectionate without an expectation that a loved one will reciprocate is even harder. But being affectionate and tender doesn't always require an immediate response. Telling your partner you love them and not expecting to hear it in return is an example of selfless affection. You are freely expressing your feelings with your partner without pushing or forcing them to do the same in return. Much of our tenderness and affection plant seeds for the future. Loved ones may be unable to reciprocate immediately because they're hurting and need us to help them overcome it. Maybe they're exhausted and they need more time to recover before they can return affection. Giving our partners affection is an investment in the long-term health of our relationships.

The gift of affection reminds our loved ones that we care. As human beings, we're strange creatures. We can often put up a wall of toughness, pretending we don't need love and affection, but when it's given, we certainly don't object - we welcome it, and feel giddy when we get it. Like everyone else, our loved ones always welcome our efforts of affection even when they aren't immediately receptive to them. And so learn to shower each other with affection. It is something that will always be welcomed with open arms.

*"They're waiting and wanting affection...
even when they're not receptive to it."*

Chapter 18

Vulnerability is a Choice

Many people like to pretend the world can't affect them. By constantly projecting an image of invulnerability and invincibility, some people can actually begin to believe that it's true. Even though most of us know it's a lie, we can strut around as if we don't have a care in the world, as if we're indifferent to how others treat us. Even if others think we don't care, our hearts are cold and numb, we feel the hurt from slurs and criticisms aimed at us — especially when it comes from our loved ones.

In an attempt to avoid hurting and feeling susceptible, some people numb themselves to their feelings. In doing this, they also anesthetize themselves to life's abundant joys. By numbing themselves to pain, they end up pushing loved ones away. By protecting themselves and pretending they can't be hurt, they convey the impression that their loved ones don't matter to them.

Sometimes the best gift we can give loved ones is to be vulnerable and sensitive to the hurts they've inflicted on us. By showing them that they can hurt us and can impact our emotions, we give them a sense of security that comes from feeling that they're a crucial part of our emotional world. Being defenseless isn't being needy, clingy, fearful, or unable to deal with emotions. Rather, it's a willingness and desire to make another person an essential part of our world, a preparedness to be hurt in order to make them understand how much they matter to us.

Learning to be vulnerable is difficult because it requires us to put ourselves in situations where we can be hurt and rejected at any moment. We put ourselves in the line of fire because we realize our loved ones' frustrations or fears are caused by their struggle to overcome their inner hurts. We *let* them affect us. (Ouch!) We let our loved ones influence us because, in allowing ourselves to be hurt, we share our honest, raw selves. Any pretense that a loved one can't hurt us implies that their feelings don't matter.

Sharing our vulnerabilities, fears and doubts, frees our loved ones from doing the same to us. When we stop trying to hide behind a mask of indifference, they begin to see us in a new light—as equally-vulnerable, fragile, human beings. They see us as susceptible to being hurt - just as they are. They see how we struggle and fear the same things. This kind of sharing allows us to feel less isolated and alone with our fears and doubts. It shows we can relate to one another, that we're connected by heartstrings.

By becoming vulnerable with one another, we allow each other to unravel our real selves so that we could both love our flaws, weaknesses, as well as our unlimited potential. We convey that we trust them with our feelings. And when others share their doubts, worries or fears (their anger and frustrations, too) we need to be more cautious and sensitive to the way we treat them. When they show their vulnerabilities, it is important to remember that *they are vulnerable to how we treat them.*

When a loved one is frustrated (especially when it concerns us), it is easy to forget they are trying to share themselves and we should try to remain as patient and respectful as possible. It is important to remember that more often than not they are feeling vulnerable and sensitive, and so they might be prone to hurt.

They are vulnerable with us, and we are vulnerable with them because we care about each other. The reason why we hurt so much, and why we want to share frustration with them is because they're important to us; they wouldn't affect us as much if we didn't care about them. Too many of us take this truth for granted. Some people think that when loved ones share or complain that they're criticizing and attacking us; in truth, they may simply be struggling with previously-unexpressed hurts we've innocently or callously inflicted. They may be struggling so much, unable to deal with their frustration, that they come across as threatening and inadvertently saying things that might hurt us. To show vulnerability is to show trust. Learning to show vulnerability and be respectful during these moments is how we build trust.

People often wrongly think that showing vulnerability is revealing weakness. But is being willing to confront and embrace our hurts, rather than numbing ourselves because we're too scared to deal with them, really a weakness? Is it a flaw to be willing to bear the brunt of criticism, frustration, and anger from loved ones, in order to understand the cause of their emotional pain?

Rather than weakness, this reflects strength. So is being willing to share less-than-noble feelings, despite the shame it carries. Society perpetuates the idea that suffering in silence, being numb to emotions, is a sign of strength, and that when men weep or share their pain, they're being effeminate. Men are expected to feel no pain or fear, but when they withdraw and aren't willing to share, they're perceived as being insensitive or emotionless. Learning these kinds of expectations and perceptions come early in life. I know I did. As a child, I was taught not to get emotional. We're told things like, *"Quiet down." "Man up." "Don't cry." "Walk it off."* All these words are meant to encourage us; instead they instill the notion that we shouldn't embrace our emotions.

Despite trying to be as caring and protective as we can be as parents, sometimes we carry with us outdated and worn-out beliefs that we unknowingly pass onto our children and loved ones. We can try to force them to fit certain expectations, and when they don't we get frustrated or disappointed. Sometimes we have these expectations of ourselves, like feeling we need to avoid expressing our vulnerabilities so that we don't come across as weak, expecting to always be in control of ourselves. After all, who is supposed to be the rock in the relationship? Right—we are.

We think projecting strength is the answer. But it frequently backfires. Soon everyone begins to think of us as strong, and when the time comes when we need to lean on someone and share, others aren't receptive to us. Their "anchor of security" seems to be coming unmoored, and that makes our loved ones feel less protected.

Learning to show vulnerability is a true display of strength. We should let our loved ones know how they affect us and, even though we feel our emotions, we aren't at their mercy. Emotions dictate how we feel, but they don't have to dictate how we act. It's better to feel the fear or hurt, act, and share ourselves anyway.

Emotional control is also a skill many of us learn in our lives. Some of us learn earlier than others (frequently, because we had to deal with a major hardship and learned emotional control as a way to deal with it). To experience deeper and meaningful relationships, we need to learn to loosen those controls and know when to choose to be vulnerable. We need to realize we are not always meant to be in control, and that it is all right to share our vulnerabilities.

This took me some time to realize all these. Just like my father, I spent my youth pretending to be strong. I didn't know any other way, and didn't know what being vulnerable meant. Much of it had to do with coming to terms with myself and accepting who I was. I had to learn to accept my failures, weaknesses and limitations, and choose whether to keep having the same recurring struggles they brought me or own up to them.

A limitation is only a constraint when we are

not willing to do something about it. Here is what I did. I sat down and wrote out all my accomplishments to date, the many struggles that had come my way, and the many small (even seemingly trivial) milestones that littered my path of personal development and growth. Then I wrote down all the weaknesses I have, the many challenges that still lay ahead and why I am daunted by them. Then, I shared all of this with two people. Through this exercise, I learned when I share my insecurities and fears it allows my loved ones to see another side of me that makes me much more approachable. They become more willing to open up as well and feel more connected with me.

Take a chance and share just one of your inner most secrets, fears or insecurities, and you'll be surprised how much your loved ones will open up. You'll learn just how the willingness to be vulnerable can build a connection and closeness with those we love.

"We let them know we're vulnerable

so they know how much they matter to us."

Chapter 19

Apologizing Isn't Weakness

When our loved ones hurt us, we question their intentions, whether they love, care for, and understand us. We wonder if their bitter, harsh words are expressed because they're hurting, or if they're meant as deliberate attacks. Either way, when others hurt us, we expect them to apologize. We all want others (especially our loved ones) to notice their wrongdoing and how they've hurt us. Whether they do it intentionally or innocently, all we want is for them to acknowledge what they've done.

An apology means admitting we've been wrong; it acknowledges and affirms our partners' right to their present feelings. We give them permission to feel hurt and to know that their feelings and the person they are matter.

But too many of us struggle with apologies. We think that by expressing regret we admit we were wrong, and that it's a sign of weakness. The notion that saying "I'm sorry" reflects a sign of weakness is flawed. What is a sign of weakness? It's not apologizing but the need to be constantly apologetic. It reflects a poor self-image and a need to please others, mostly to avoid confrontation. The inability to apologize, to admit having been wrong, to claim ignorance of our own foibles is also a weakness. It reflects a low sense of pride and self-esteem that we're desperate to protect.

What is weakness, at its base? It's just another area we haven't mastered yet. It's an area where we feel vulnerable and doubt ourselves.

We've all wronged someone. We've all been insensitive, because of pride, stubbornness or ignorance. We've defended ourselves, even at the cost of the well-being and feelings of our partners. Sometimes our loved ones just need us to apologize so they can feel we're still connected, we understand their frustration and hurt. When we're unable to recognize that a simple apology is all they need, we add to the hurt and frustration. What started as a simple problem, misgiving or misunderstanding, where an apology would have sufficed, becomes something hotly contested, and brews the question, "Do you even care how I feel?" If we're unwilling to apologize, we reject their feelings of hurt and frustration; therefore, we're perceived as rejecting them. Because they feel rejected, they begin to question our love for them.

Relationships are about nurturing, supporting, and encouraging each other. They are based on trust, love, respect, tolerance, and attempts at understanding. Although these statements seem self-evident, how many of us *truly live* by these values?

The sad truth is we all get confused. This can create problems that become more daunting than they need to be. At times, we overlook and discount tools and insights because of their simplicity. Even worse, we think we've mastered them already, or we aren't willing to admit our shortcomings, so we pretend these essentials don't really matter. Other times, we believe we're perfectly fine and aligned, that it's our loved ones who need to change, that it is they who need to accommodate our needs, our unique personalities and beliefs. But, have we ever considered that our loved ones may be thinking the same thing!

As the old adage goes, we try to change everything around us without first looking at ourselves. We're the causality and catalyst in our lives. If you take the time to notice, you'll see that all of your problems have a unique, singular element in common: *you*.

A loving and healthy relationship isn't a battle for the high ground, a battle between ego and pride—and it definitely isn't a battle to establish who's right and who's wrong. The notion that one party has to be wrong for the other to be right is flawed and incomplete. There's a third alternative: a misunderstanding, or how our views of the world differ.

If we can learn to let go of the notion that we need to be right, or that apologizing is an admission of fault, we begin to see that love doesn't require battles. We don't need to wage war. We don't feel the need to get our point across, or take a stand because we can't let our partners "win." When we stop viewing loved ones as enemies and begin to see them as human beings who are struggling with their own fears and feelings, we'll understand that sometimes they'll inadvertently hurt us.

It can be hard to see this when emotions are raw. Partners can often get hurt in the crossfire when trying to express themselves. We know we've hurt each other, we can see it in each other's faces and in each other's tears, but we persist and carry on ruthlessly, continuing to push until we feel our point is accurately made. We can go into trance-like states when trying to make points, becoming arrogant and stubborn. By taking an obstinate stand, we don't realize that our partners may have misunderstood what we said, or that we may have misinterpreted the entire situation. We're so busy being right we don't notice where we may be wrong. We may be making a point about something completely unrelated to the real issue, just to make a point, C'mon, fess up — this has happened to you a time or two, right?

When we assume this tactic, many of us would rather deny our faults than admit them. Our pride won't let us confess. It becomes more a matter of preserving our egos than it is of trying to understand our loved ones, trying to ease their worries and pain.

At times, we can also be trying to teach someone a lesson. Maybe we feel the need to take a stand for our rights and feelings so they won't think—or feel--they can mistreat or walk all over us. We don't want to be their doormats, so we dig in with our heels and make our rights heard, even when it means hurting our partners. But here's the point: Are we really taking a stand against *them*?

For some people, the idea of apologizing means allowing our partners to mistreat us, to be willing to tolerate less than we deserve. The fact that we feel the need to take a stand for our rights, fighting and belittling loved ones in the process, implies that we're fearful of being mistreated. We may be questioning whether we feel deserving in the first place. We take a stand for our rights at the cost of feeling unloved. We take a stand for them to love us because we aren't sure they do.

When our loved ones are doing the belittling, it's frustrating to think they are hurting us and yet they are incapable of seeing it. Stubbornness creates a rift in relationships. The more someone hurts us, the greater the chasm widens. Here's the lesson: *If we can accept how we affect another person's feelings, the necessary changes in the relationship can be made so both parties feel more fulfilled emotionally.*

The first step in solving any relationship problem or challenge is to admit there's a problem, and figure out each person's role in perpetuating it. But we all struggle to think about relationship challenges, and can neglect following through with solutions. Maybe it's because the fix seems so simple. We may think the fix is so obvious and simple that our loved ones should notice it first. Some people aren't willing to acknowledge fault unless their loved ones admit their wrongdoings first. We aren't willing to admit we're hurting them, because they aren't willing to admit they're hurting us.

In cases like these it seems a score card is being kept — one on which we constantly tally our loved ones' faults without taking note of our own. The truth is that we tend to forget the wrongs we've done in the past. We forget all the little things that have been said out of frustration, which were overly harsh and hurtful. We never really notice how much we contribute to our loved ones' hurt — *but they do*. They remember almost every slight against them; they remember all the times we said a hurtful word or did something insensitive.

No one can remember every little instance in which we've been thoughtless with words. No one can know all the words or actions that hurt our loved ones. It may be because our loved ones hide their hurt, withdraw, and don't mention the slights. It might be because we're too distracted or carried away in the moment.

Our loved ones won't always remember the hurts they've inflicted, nor can we expect them to. We all hurt those we love from time to time, mostly unintentionally. Our hope is that there is enough vested love and care that we'll be given the benefit of the doubt. We hope our loved ones will realize we may not always be elegant word smiths; we may not always know what to say or do, but throughout our relationship with them, we've showed enough care and appreciation to apologize, and allow them to forgive us and see the true intention behind it all: our sincere attempts at loving and understanding them.

And sometimes, there may be more than one reason to apologize. It isn't always because we've done something wrong. At times, it's just that we don't understand why and how a loved one is hurting, even though we earnestly want to ease it. We apologize because we care, and are attempting to show our loved ones we're trying to understand and share their grief.

Oftentimes, an apology is an attempt to avoid a confrontation if we feel we'll become the target of judgment or criticism. No one wants to hear harsh words directed against them, so we may use an apology to avoid hurtful hostilities or as a plea to stop being criticized.

There is an area where apologies can be counterproductive and can actually bolster hurt and distrust: apologizing to escape responsibility. When apologies are made to evade responsibility, they cause more problems later on. We may overuse apologies in an attempt to please, but then not do anything to rectify the poor behavior that led to problems in the first place. Simply saying "I'm sorry" and then not doing anything about what happened doesn't cut it. There's no expectation that the problems or bad habits will disappear overnight, but a genuine effort at overcoming them needs to be perceived. We need to make a proactive attempt to make a positive difference. If we just apologize and do nothing, expecting our loved ones to continue to tolerate our poor behavior, it will eventually reach a tipping point when they'll begin to turn away because we will have destroyed their trust in us.

When we ask for forgiveness, it should come from a genuine desire to please or cease to offend others. For men, an apology is frequently used to avoid what seems to be an unnecessary conflict. A lot of men will express regret to stop criticisms, accusations, and blame being thrown their way by their loved ones. But if the apology fails, they may withdraw into silence to preserve their self-esteem and confidence. Consequently, the withdrawal often spurs loved ones to more elevated levels of frustration. If words and tone become even harsher, they may withdraw further, which only serves to make it impossible to resolve the issue.

While many of us might complain about our partner's lack of emotional maturity, we can fail to realize that she/he is also pointing his/her finger at us. We can be guilty of the same things we complain about because we may lack in the same areas. It is important to keep our eyes on ourselves first, and when we've hurt a loved one, to know when and how to apologize.

"The gift of apology:

acknowledging how our actions affect others

and a sincere desire to ease pain."

Chapter 20

From Listening To Understanding

When it comes to communicating with partners, many people listen with the intent of sharing their own feelings rather than trying to understand the other person's perspective. It can happen on our end as well; though we may be listening, are we truly present with them? If as we're listening we're waiting to share, to express our opinions, we aren't truly being present. How can we be truly present if we're constantly inside our own heads?

Listening is an art. By actively listening, engaging, and asking for feedback and clarity, we can better understand loved ones' feelings, and help them to feel their opinions and voices matter. There are times when our minds wander off, even though we know we need to be present. If work is piling up or a project's due date is approaching, it's hard to focus and be there for someone. Even though it's a struggle during these times, we need to make the effort. Most of the time, the effort is enough because listening isn't just about hearing what others say, but allowing enough time for them to feel they're being heard.

Listening is a gift. When someone rejects our thoughts we share, it's as if they're telling us our thoughts and opinions don't matter. We all want to feel we're understood and that our frustration matters. Actively listening and being present when others' share their concerns comforts them, letting them feel they are understood.

When loved ones share their hurts, frustrations and concerns, a desire can swell inside us where we feel compelled to try helping them fix the situation or offer suggestions on how to solve their problems. The first thought that can pop into our mind is: How can I fix this? How can I ease the problem? We put on our handyman overalls and launch into "fix it" mode, trying to sort out and solve the issue. We think we're doing the right thing in offering advice and workable solutions. But sometimes, despite our efforts and the advice we offer, our loved one remains frustrated and annoyed, and eventually they become frustrated with us. We can become the scapegoats for their frustration, even though we're trying to help. With emotions flaring, they end up yelling at us, declaring we don't understand; that we don't care how they feel.

At this point, many of us can feel our own anger and frustration rising, thinking our loved ones are being ungrateful and unappreciative of our attempts to help. Of course we care; we wouldn't have offered advice if we didn't; we wouldn't have risked and sat through the emotional discourse if we didn't care. No one would offer advice if they didn't care. And anyone who loves their partner would want to try to solve their problems to end his or her pain.

At one time, this is what I thought.

Frequently, in my attempts to show care and concern, I offered feedback and potential solutions but still, others' frustrations with me seemed to escalate. Then I got frustrated myself because I felt unappreciated. I got even more frustrated when it seemed my partner would complain about the same set of problems over and over again. Each time I'd try to fix it, and we'd end up arguing, seething with frustration and hurt.

I felt she was ungrateful of my attempts to help. She felt I was unwilling to hear her out completely, which made her feel that she couldn't share with me. I was too much in "fix-it mode" to see that what she may have really wanted. I initially blamed her for attacking me, but it wasn't really her fault—it was a simple case of getting things in the wrong order. I was trying to fix the problem before easing her worries and allowing her to feel heard.

Sometimes what others want at that moment is a sympathetic ear. Sometimes they just need to vent. Offering advice may be our language of love, but if we deny them the opportunity to get their feelings out, they may feel all we are trying to do is to fix the problem, not because we care, but just to get over it. They may not feel they were able to fully express themselves. They can feel as if we see their concerns as unwanted burdens because if we did care, we would have taken the time to fully understand their plight, right?

This is the simple difference between what a loved one really *needs* and what we may be prone to do in a situation that may cause unnecessary hurts. Giving advice, trying to fix things, is of secondary importance. The things we need to do — first and foremost — is to ensure our loved ones feel listened to and to let them know we care. Denying them time to share actually denies their feelings.

Sometimes, all we want is for someone to hear out our thoughts. And that listening well is more than enough to make us feel better. Advice is great, but the assurance that we were heard and that we matter is far better.

And for others to feel in this manner, we need to actively listen. This means really hearing what the other person might be saying, and not saying. Its more than just wanting to relate what they are telling us. It means developing the ability to read genuine, behind-the-scenes feelings to decipher what it is they're really trying to say.

When our partners are the ones doing the listening, we hope they know us well enough to be able to sift through what might be convoluted confusion and hear what we mean. But they may not, and they may respond in ways that sound abrasive, confronting, or argumentative, especially if the discussion is about the relationship. Sometimes there are meanings behind these kinds of responses. Here are examples with one possible interpretation of what each statement could mean: If we are truly paying attention to our loved ones and by actively listening, then we'll be able to decipher their implied messages.

1. You don't love me. = I feel somewhat neglected by you.

2. Why don't you ever take me out? = It feels as

if you're ashamed of me.

3. Why can't you just listen to me? = It doesn't seem like you care about my feelings or thoughts.

4. Don't tell me what to do. = You don't seem to trust me.

5. Why can't you just give me some space? = Despite loving you, I feel suffocated right now and need to gather my thoughts.

6. I want (need) some time alone. = I'm struggling with my own problems and need time to heal.

7. It's not you, it's me. = It just doesn't feel like you understand me.

8. Why can't you just do what I tell you to? = It doesn't seem like you respect my feelings.

9. Please shut up! = Can you stop attacking me and making me feel terrible?

10. Why are you always so negative? = It seems you always treat yourself poorly and expect me to make you feel better.

11. Why are you trying to change me? = Am I not good enough for you?

12. When will you propose to me? = I need to know if you love me and time is ticking away (I'm not getting any younger).

13. I want a child with you. = I want to build a family with you and have a little "us" running around.

14. Let's get a pet. = I want to test whether you're willing to commit to me.

15. Why are you looking at that woman? = I feel you don't find me as attractive as her, or as attractive as I was before.

16. Why don't you just get a job? = I'm uncertain about the future and need some stability if we're going to stay together. I need someone who I know can take care of and support me, both emotionally and financially.

17. Why can't you just grow up? = I feel like I have to worry about everything on my own.

18. Why don't you change clothes (or lose weight, get fit, wear make-up, etc.)? = I don't feel you're putting in as much effort as before and it seems you are taking me for granted.

19. Can't you clean-up after yourself? = I feel like your parent; you don't see how much I have to deal with without you compounding the challenge.

20. What do you want from me? = It seems like everything I do is criticized or not appreciated.

There is a world behind words. There may easily be a deeper meaning behind any sentence spoken within a relationship. When we learn to truly listen to others, to read between the lines, then we can safely navigate through the minefields in a relationship. We become better problem solvers, better lovers and better protectors mainly due to becoming better listeners. We see things the way we're expected to see them from our loved ones' perspectives.

With a better understanding of what active listening entails, let's delve into why it's so hard to engage in it. There are plenty of reasons:

- Active listening can be difficult when we're overly-concerned about protecting our egos. Trying to protect our egos, we distort messages; we become biased. We come into conversations with our own assumptions long before we engage in listening. At times, when we're hurt, we can become overly-sensitive to criticism and presumed attacks and confuse neutral statements with antagonism. We can assume our loved ones' frustrations are attacks on us, when they may not be. Every skill becomes rusty through lack of use. Active listening is no different. The less often we use it, the worse our abilities to understand loved ones' emotional subtext will become.

- We are more concerned about listening with the intent of contributing, of sharing our perspective or insights, than simply listening so the other person feels fully heard and understood. This might be because we're projecting our own opinions and thoughts, assuming we already know what they're trying to say or how they feel without taking the time and effort to truly understand. We develop incomplete or misleading conclusions, without hearing them out. When we're too focused on expressing ourselves, we become distracted from being truly present with loved ones.

- Maybe we're too busy drowning out our partners by distracting ourselves with something else: the news, television or work. We need to start paying closer attention. When we're too focused on personal fulfillment, our ability to be present declines, tainting our ability to hear subtle (and not so subtle) cries of pain.

Active listening is the glue that makes our relationship efforts work. It lets our partner know they're loved, and that all our efforts are attempts to convey how much we love them. The next time someone shares their feelings and thoughts, ask yourself: *"Am I hearing their words—or am I just listening so I can share mine?"*

Learning to do this helps others feel they can share openly and honestly without being criticized or retaliated against. They become more appreciative of our listening ears and are more willing to listen to us. Active listening is a gift; it shows that we matter to others, and they matter to us.

"Listening isn't hearing with our ears;

it's hearing with our hearts."

Chapter 21

How We Misunderstand

How does it feel when your partner truly understands you? Some describe it as a sense of belonging. Others say it makes them feel loved and cared for. Still others describe it as finding their other half. However you describe it, I bet it includes feeling in sync with your partner and s/he feels the same. At times, we may not need to utter a single word because others already know what to do, what to say, and how to comfort us.

Being understood is immeasurably powerful. We all want to understand and be understood by our loved ones. But because confusion and misunderstanding can happen when we share our fears and feelings, being able to truly understand another person can seem somewhat mystical. Many books explain how to understand loved ones better; each offer various models and insights, but we may still struggle to try and fully understand each other. The entire notion of understanding may not focus on understanding at all; it might be focused on *being understood* — the desire to have our feelings and thoughts truly experienced by another. This need is a desire for validation; it's proof that we matter, that our feelings, thoughts, opinions and beliefs are palpable to loved ones.

As we look around, we notice that some people have a more developed intuitive sense—a superior grasp on empathy—while others struggle when trying to understand others, trying their best to make sense of everything. Those who rationalize may think they lack empathy, but do they? We tend to think that those who don't have empathy, or are unable to understand how we feel, are insensitive or lack the ability to care about others. But is this actually insensitivity—or something else we haven't considered?

It may just be that rationalizers approach emotions differently and this is what causes conflict. Some feel the need to suppress and avoid their emotions (which can make them seem cold, indifferent or uncaring) to be able to think. They may feel their emotions keep them from thinking clearly, and that they need to calm themselves down before they can share and let others in.

Others use their emotions as guiding compasses to steer their decisions, helping them know what to do. They use emotions to make decisions because they feel their emotions are the most accurate indicators of how to live life. But what happens when loved ones suppress their emotions, as doggedly as partners embrace expressing them?

There will be problems, misunderstandings, and pain, because we don't understand each other. Neither way is better than the other. It's our expectation that they should understand things from our point view is unreasonable. The difference in how we approach emotions can cause massive rifts in relationships is summed up in these two statements:

> *"I act therefore I feel."*
>
> *"I feel therefore I act."*

We need to develop tolerance for other ways of reaching decisions and conclusions. When loved ones hurt us, some of us tend to think they're doing it intentionally. We expect them to realize on their own that they're hurting us and, if they don't, we decide they must not care about us.

This isn't so because we can't always understand where our loved ones are coming from. Each person comes with a wealth of experiences and beliefs that are unique to him/her. Unless we embrace this, we'll always *expect* loved ones to understand us with little effort on our part. We'll think that what we believe and how we feel should be obvious to the other person. This isn't always the case.

Instead, learning to understand each other better is a journey of discovering and rediscovering ourselves and our loved ones. It begins with the simple willingness to engage, share and embrace each other's points of view. Just because they view things differently doesn't mean they're wrong. So often, there is no right or wrong, only differences in the ways we view the world based on our past experiences.

I grew up thinking that others should view emotions the way I did – that you can't trust them. In my past relationships, I was the one who came from an objective place, and my partners from a more emotional place. This difference caused many hurtful moments. Over time, I learned that not trusting my emotions had more to do with insecurities stemming from my past, and that to better understand others I needed to better understand why I came to distrust my emotions in the first place.

The truth is, no one will ever understand us completely, no matter how much we share. No one can feel the same pain we feel. When we are cut, no one is going to feel the cold blade against our skin. When we are tormented by bullies, labeled hurtful and harsh names, no one is going to feel the same sting we feel. No sharing ever amounts to having lived through the experience.

Take time to share each other's views of the world, and when you do, realize that any misunderstanding may simply be a difference in views based on our life experiences. We won't always understand others, and need to let it go at that, with love.

"There is no such thing as black or white – only differences and unexplored terrains."

Chapter 22

Forgive but Don't Forget

It's natural to make mistakes. Everyone makes them. It's how we learn. It's also how we become who we are and how we become better people. It is through trial and error that we learn to walk, speak, and write. Everything we learn, every skill we obtain, is through trial and error. Sometimes we succeed quickly; other times, we struggle—some things take longer and require more effort.

Some of us are gifted enough to pick up skills faster than others. Not all people learn at the same rate or possess the same strengths. Many people excel at one skill set and are challenged by others. Sometimes those who seem to have excelled quickly may, in fact, have struggled; it may just be that they spent more time mastering the skill. They put more effort into developing it. Whatever the case, the ability to learn is in all of us.

Like everyone else, we make mistakes. And when we do, we hope our loved ones will recognize our efforts and desire to learn from them. We also hope they'll forgive us when we make them. Like us, our loved ones won't always make sound judgments; they'll occasionally say and do hurtful things. And like us, our loved ones also want to be forgiven when they make mistakes. After all, the mistakes are usually attempts at becoming better people.

Many times when we make mistakes, we can defend ourselves when our loved ones are aggravated with our efforts. When this happens, we can feel like we have no room to move, no leeway, and feel suffocated. We begin to feel that they expect us to succeed every single time we try. It feels as if we're expected to be perfect, that every mistake we make disappoints them.

Without a tolerance for mistakes, love can't survive. Appreciation can't be fostered, and it can lead to unwillingness to try again. If we fail and hurt our partners and they retaliate, it makes us withdraw. We seem to expect our partners to grant us leeway, but how many of us struggle with granting them the same!

One area where I've wanted this kind of leeway relates to my communication skills. In the past, I've been someone who used to struggle to express himself. I went out of my comfort zone and took a job in sales to get more comfortable talking with all kinds of people and learning the art of conversation. I also challenged myself to go to networking events so I could strike up conversations with people I didn't know, and learn to better present myself.

When it comes to sharing my insecurities and weaknesses, I've also challenged myself to go out of my comfort zone because I want to offer more of myself to others. It still terrifies me; it's something I still struggle with, but the more I do it, the easier it gets.

It's inevitable that when we go out of our comfort zones, we'll make mistakes, and will want to correct them. When our loved ones make mistakes, they will want to do the same. Although in relationships it can be tricky. While no one wants to continuously hurt those they care about, there are times we do. At certain times, it isn't a matter of whether they hurt us; it's a matter of whether they're trying to *love* us. If they make a mistake, do they try to correct it? We should be quick to forgive them when they're willing to learn from their mistakes.

How many of us let our fears and insecurities hurt our loved ones, so they don't feel they can safely share with us? How many of us feel that over time they withdraw their love from us to the point where they're willing to leave us to our struggles and pain, rather than try to ease them? How many of us let our relationships die silent deaths because we aren't willing to tolerate our partners' failings?

I've seen the unwillingness to forgive first hand. I watched it rip my parents' marriage apart. My mother constantly brought up my father's past faults, even though it happened decades and decades ago. This made him feel unworthy and unloved. The same thing happened to me in my past relationships. In fights, my partner would bring up past wrongdoings that had hurt her. It felt like she used them as tools of guilt, making me feel worthless and undeserving, incapable of loving another person, and like a constant failure in the relationship.

Frequently, I ran away from such relationships. I wanted someone with whom I could start afresh. At least with a new relationship, my past wrongdoings wouldn't be brought up. This made me a serial dater. I did learn to open up, and become a better partner, but I made plenty of mistakes along the way. Many times I left relationships because I wasn't able to receive the much needed forgiveness I needed. Being young and foolish at the time, I didn't realize the reason they didn't forgive me was because I wasn't able to forgive them. I wasn't willing to let them fail, to make mistakes. I wasn't compassionate enough to realize they needed to feel safe to make mistakes in order to grow as a person.

Wouldn't you love to be able to turn to your partner and say whatever you feel without the fear of being attacked or misunderstood? Wouldn't you want him or her to listen to your hurts even when you're just rambling or venting, without feeling judged or guilty?

No matter what we do, no matter how fulfilling and satisfying our relationships are, hurting each other will always be a part of them. Hurt within a relationship is a sign for us to stop, look, and listen. It is a time to dive inside and figure out where the cause of the hurt lies. But, instead of realizing the hurt is inside us—perhaps an unresolved past hurt or fear—we can blame it on our loved ones. We can think they are cause of the pain, not realizing they're innocent. We may not see they have triggered an unresolved hurt in ourselves, and that when we attack, we not only push them away but the pain they triggered. When we hurt each other, we need to look at why we did it in the first place.

Often relationship pain comes about when we express our opinions without realizing the possible repercussions they can have. We share, hoping our loved ones will give us the benefit of the doubt and that what we say won't be taken harshly, despite our poor choice of words. But there are also instances where our partners hurt us and aren't willing to acknowledge and correct their misbehavior. This is when we need to think seriously about whether they truly care.

If our loved ones know they've hurt us and understand their actions were unreasonable, what are they doing to correct the behavior? Offer them forgiveness when they make mistakes, but not when they have malicious intent. If they're unwilling to change the behavior that hurts us, understand the reason why. Are we being unreasonable in our requests? Do they feel their needs are being sacrificed for ours and we're unable to recognize it? Or, are they unwilling to accept their responsibility in the matter? Can we sense that loved ones making genuine efforts to change for the better, to love us better, or are they just doing what suits them, disregarding our well-being?

For the most part, our loved ones do, indeed, care about us. But forgiveness doesn't mean forgetting or continuing to tolerate poor behavior. We forgive our loved ones because they're trying to love us; however, it doesn't mean we should tolerate them when they're mistreating us. Forgiving gives them the opportunity to grow and prove they've mended their ways because they can see how what they did adversely affects us. Forgiveness gives them breathing space to realize what they did wrong.

They might not completely fix or mend their ways, but they're taking seriously their efforts to improve.

It's hard, but once we decide to forgive, we must let go of the past. It isn't about forgetting the hurt; it's about refusing to use the past as ammunition during future conflicts. We shouldn't hold onto past wrongdoings, we shouldn't keep repeating how much we've been hurt. Revisiting past hurts isn't forgiveness.

Revisiting the past is the same as using guilt as a form of control and manipulation. Our loved ones will feel we're using past guilt to justify hurting them from that day forward. When we drudge up the past, our loved ones will only feel as if we have a vindictive desire to continue to make them feel as hurt as we were, and still are, by a past transgression.

No one wants their past wrongdoings, or moments of weakness, to be forever held over their heads, waiting to be dropped whenever another argument ensues. We don't want that from our partners, and they don't want it from us. So, when we decide to forgive, we must remember that we're foregoing our right to use the memory against them at any time in the future. And, when we give forgiveness, it must be in a way that they won't feel attacked. Even though we may be frustrated or hurt by their actions, we must not retaliate. We'll let them know that what they did was hurtful, but that we also know they didn't want to hurt us. Forgiveness is about letting them know that we simply want them to change their behavior because it hurts us. This is what the gift of forgiveness is all about.

"When we forgive, we forego our right to use past transgressions as tools of guilt."

Chapter 23

Feel Their Pain

Life's journey is filled with many ups and downs. Every day there are unfortunate incidents on the news: tragic stories of accidents that kill entire families, random shootings, and teens speeding and killing themselves or crippling loved ones. Most of the time, these incidents don't directly affect us or the people we care about.

Whenever we hear about a tragedy, we breathe a sigh of relief because it didn't affect us; then we keep on living life as usual. With each passing day, when nothing out of the ordinary occurs — no unfortunate accidents, no family member being stricken with a disease, no one we know losing their job — we begin to take days without pain and fear for granted. We forget that a day without worry is a blessed day indeed.

As much as we hope and pray that nothing terrible will ever happen to us or our loved ones, fate doesn't always comply. Life is filled with as many challenges as it is with happiness and joy. Rainy days are normal. Certain realties and events are inescapable and often unavoidable, no matter how much we may try to remove them from our daily thoughts. Few like to entertain the idea that something unfortunate will eventually happen. We can pretend and hope it won't, but sooner or later it will.

We're mortal; we are susceptible to disease, illness, age, accidents, and dying. Someone will eventually suffer a tragedy or die: a child before his/her time or an elderly parent who has lived a full and prosperous life. Accidents and death are integral parts of life. This reality should make us even more appreciative of what we have. This should remind us to be grateful for our loved ones and compassionate toward everyone else.

No matter what we do, there will be times when situations spiral out of control and no matter what we do, we can't change the outcome. At these times, some blame others; sometimes, we blame ourselves and absorb guilt. In hindsight, everything seems so much clearer - if only we hadn't done this, if only we'd noticed that, but we didn't. We can't always expect to be vigilant, to always know what's around the corner. Something awful has happened — someone we loved deeply — has died, and all we can do is grieve. No amount of taking it out on others, and amount of hurting ourselves will change this.

When someone dies, all we can do is cry, and perhaps isolate ourselves to mourn, because many times just getting out of bed may feel insurmountable. At such times, all we may have is regret, wishing we'd said we were sorry for hurting them, or told them how much we loved and appreciated them. They may simply have needed us to let them know we forgave them, to bless them with the much-needed solace they craved.

In times of pain, we need to be able to give consolation, which is the act of giving comfort and emotional support. It's letting others lean on us to cry and pour open their hearts as they wish. It's letting them know they aren't all alone in their pain. Even though we may not truly understand or feel our loved ones' grief, we want them to share it with us. Such moments are precious. Too many of us let others struggle with losses in isolation. Pain isn't something to be ashamed of. It's human; it's inside all of us.

The death of my first real friend, Khang, left me devastated. For me, it was a time of emotional rage. My resilience, my thickened shell, and all the years of learning to numb myself came undone. I vividly remember the day of his funeral; I gave his eulogy on behalf of his friends. It was the first time I ever spoke publicly, and the first time I had cried since I was ten years old.

After a tragedy, such as the death of close friend, we become susceptible to the other people's words. Comments that are off, which would normally not affect us can directly hit our hearts and bring us down. This happened at the funeral. My parents were never elegant with their words - far from it - that day was no exception. When my father saw me in such an emotional state, he jokingly said, "I hope you cry as much for me at my funeral." Like a tap, I closed my heart, and seethed with resentment and bitterness toward my father. My mother didn't say anything. It took many years to come to terms with the experience so I can forgive my parents for their insensitivity. I realize they never intended to hurt me. That day, I just wish they had been able to comfort and share the hurt with me.

When tragedy strikes, it can send us into a tailspin of depression. One that would be very difficult to escape from. This may lead to unhealthy forms of relief: alcohol, fleeting romances with strangers, the alluring life of drugs and adrenaline, or getting lost in our work to the point that we don't feel anything at all. These are attempts to survive and feel alive again, to remind us there's a reason to live and that another's person's death isn't the end of our own lives. For others, these are attempts to numb the pain, to provide just enough strength so we can take each new day as it comes. Whatever it is, we're all trying to come to terms with mortality and our susceptibility to life's ever-changing landscape.

When faced with tragedies, it can feel like a scorching knife has been plunged into the pit of our stomachs, and our chests cave in where no amounts of words can adequately express the pain we're feeling. No matter what anyone says, even the sweetest words will not be enough. In times like these we need a friend or someone to mourn with us, to share our pain and grief. Sharing is somehow less painful than bearing a loss in bleak isolation. It still hurts, but at least we have someone to share it with.

With simple caring words, simple moments in which loved ones and friends lend their shoulders, our hurt lessens briefly. We no longer feel uniquely alone. Misery loves company, not because we want others to hurt exactly as we do (that would be impossible), but because we want someone to understand how we feel, someone to cry with us. We need someone who comprehends without us having to explain ourselves.

Imagine loved ones in such grief and pain that they seem unable to recover. These are precious moments for connecting; instances where they can't help but bare their hearts because their emotions are overflowing. We may not truly understand how they feel; their loss may even seem trivial to us. For very young children, the loss of a blanket, doll or other favorite toy is sufficient reason for torrents of grief.

Whatever the reason, when loved ones are in the throes of grief, they need us to be there for them. We need to give up our own needs and be selfless so we can truly be present for them. By foregoing our own needs, we enable them to freely share their pain. This builds trust; they realize they'll be able to rely on us next time, too. But if we minimize or belittle their anguish, or criticize the legitimacy of their pain (such as bringing the conversation back to ourselves, comparing our pain with theirs), their trust will suffer a blow. Soon they'll be indifferent to us. They won't feel we deserve them at their best and most generous when we aren't willing to embrace and support them when life is at its worst.

We simply can't abandon our loved ones when trials and tragedies strike. We can't let them hurt in isolation. Every time they feel we aren't there for them, it would seem as if we don't want to be with them and, in time. Consequently, they won't want to be there for us when we need them too.

Don't do this to your loved ones. Let them

share their pain, their frustration, and their grief. They will overcome it eventually. Being there and supporting them will give them the strength to endure the process. Sometimes all they need is the courage to get through the next day.

Having someone to share pain with is therapeutic. When we see loved ones crying or hurting, a simple hug to let them know we're there can make all the difference. It will mean the world to them. Sharing hurt and pain is a gift; it's also a request to care and bond with them. It can simply be letting our loved ones know we're there and that they don't need to express their hurt for us to see it. They don't even have to share with us, or reciprocate right at that moment. Just hug them, and accept the fact that they may not have the strength to hug us back right now. Either way, whether they share or not, understand.

"Hurt with them. This is sometimes the best thing you can do. Sometimes it's the only thing you can do for them."

Chapter 24

Nurture Loved Ones' Growth

When we love someone, we want them to reach their full potential. Because we care for them, we want to help them along the way: lend a helping hand, offer a pearl of wisdom, or be their sounding board while they grapple with thoughts and emotions. We want to contribute to their growth.

Getting into a relationship (any relationship) we become responsible for another's welfare. If we become parents, we want to make sure our children grow, and this requires us to become less selfish and more selfless. Our children are on their own journeys of self-discovery; we need to be there to guide and understand them, and be generous with love and affection. As parents, we understand that as they strive to grow, they'll make innocent mistakes. We understand that when they are frustrated with us as parents; it is not with malicious intent, they are simply trying to deal with their fears, insecurities, and emotions. We need to be able to support and nurture our children in these times.

However, when our children start to mature and form their own views of the world, becoming less malleable, it can be quite challenging. It can become harder to get them to comply with our requests and expectations They may also seem to grow up too fast and that we don't feel we know them as well, especially in adolescence when they can tend to share less and less of themselves. It can feel frightening when our influence over their lives seems to dwindle, and we feel we may not be able to care for or protect them like we used to. They no longer need to rely on us like they used to because they are now able to think for themselves. Despite the fact that they may have achieved notable and worthwhile goals and we're enormously proud of them, it's easy to feel less significant, and less involved in the trajectory of their lives. The more they grow—becoming stronger, more confident and independent—the less they seek our advice and the input of others. We are unable to contribute to their well-being without being accused of "meddling" in their affairs.

As parents, we're proud to help our children grow into confident, capable teenagers and adults. We nurture their abilities, mentor them, and encourage them to strive for more. But nurturing the growth of our partners is not the same thing. It can get more complicated when our emotional needs are involved. With our partners, rather than being there to applaud their development, we can instead demand that our needs be met. We can tolerate their progression and discovery as long as we get our needs met - as long as we get our fill.

We happily invest in our children's emotional development, letting them fumble, stumble, and fall, but many people are not willing to be selfless and put their partners' needs first. How we support our partners all too often stems back to how we were supported when we were young.

As I matured, my relationship with my parents and my personal development was squelched. It seemed as though my needs were always shelved. When I got older, I wanted freedom from them. I wanted to feel like I could express myself openly and confidently, but could not do that with them. I craved their support and understanding, yet everything always seemed to be about them, how they were hurting - how my other parent had wronged them. It was as if they were constantly expecting me to support them, rather than the other way around.

My relationship with my parents instilled a strong need for freedom, which resulted in a massive fear of commitment. Whenever any of my relationships started to feel suffocating, I sensed the need to end it. This happened after a five-year relationship with my ex-fiancée. Like the feelings I had with my parents growing up, I felt like my emotional growth, well-being, and dreams were being sacrificed to satisfy her needs. I resented that her needs felt overwhelming, demanding, and ever so taxing.

At the time, I didn't realize I was reacting to deeply rooted insecurities. I felt she was unable to see I was struggling to be there for her, especially when I felt I was running on empty. I needed her help in nurturing myself too, to give me the confidence to do things like quit my dead-end job back then because I hated it so much. I needed her to comfort me as much she needed me to comfort her.

Our past experiences can lead us to problems like these that greatly affect our relationships. It can happen when we feel unsupported and unable to nurture other people's growth. We can also worry that if we pour our heart and soul into nurturing their growth, they may one day outgrow us and leave. Or we can feel that we may become unwanted burdens, and because we want to remain a part of their lives, we can sabotage their growth, at times even go as far as creating a dependent relationship – financially or emotionally – in an attempt to keep them in our lives.

We need to realize that dynamics like these are rooted in our past. When we understand this, we are able to show our loved ones that we recognize their potential, and we can help them recognize and embrace it. We are better able to give them the strength to strive, persist, and bounce back from adversity faster. We do this by letting them know they are more capable than they think, and stronger than they realize. At times, by showing our partners tough love, we are helping them make sure they will indeed reach the goals they set in life.

At the same time, it is crucial that any tough love be shown purely for their personal growth and happiness. Frustrations that we may feel regarding their progress can stem from our belief that they are not living up to their potential, or our expectations of them. Sometimes we expect a lot from them, much more that what they really want for themselves. It could also be because they doubt themselves so much that they avoid taking the next steps required to in order to flourish. *"If only you could see what I see in you and why I'm fighting so hard for you..."* could be our heartfelt plea.

Even though we may love and want to nurture our loved ones' growth, we can at times fall victim to our own pain. At such times, it can feel like they're hurting us, but we're simply reacting to our own fears. When we do this, we can fool ourselves into thinking we're showing tough love; in truth, we're trying to ease our own worries and we don't realize we're hurting them in the process. We can use tools that instill and perpetuate their fears: nagging, yelling, making threats, or using intimidation, or ultimatums. These are only some of the ways we can belittle loved ones, making them fearful and causing them to question our love.

Even though we're pushing them so they can grow, we can do it at the cost of their growth in other areas: their self-confidence, self-esteem and their ability to trust another human being. We can do it in such a way that they are left in doubt, feeling as if we're always questioning them and their worth. If they're made to feel they just don't "get it," a battle may begin. They become distant, trying to prove they don't need us and that we're in no position to dictate or judge them when, in truth, all they really want is to prove they're worthy of our full acceptance and love.

If they're treated this way, as our loved ones grow and mature they may become more defiant, opinionated, and argumentative. If they don't feel we accept them, they reject us. This is a coping mechanism in many dysfunctional relationships: we reject first so we can't be rejected.

No one else's judgment can hurt us unless we embrace it – unless we allow their input to affect our sense of self-worth. When we feel we aren't being accepted, we want to fight, defend and retaliate. We can keep trying to tell ourselves they're beneath us, so they shouldn't influence how we feel. But despite denying and pretending that loved ones can't hurt us, we desperately want their acceptance, approval and love!

This kind of dynamic doesn't instill a sense of belonging in a relationship. Tools of poor quality inflict significant damage. They make us feel as if our loved ones are people we need to fight and prove wrong. Sooner or later, we become the people they need to get away from because they feel we're holding them back. Rather than seeing us as comrades who want to encourage their growth, they see us as saboteurs who are limiting them, their appreciation for themselves, and life in general.

By learning to nurture each other's growth, we help them develop the tools they need to nurture us in return. No one likes to be on the receiving end of nagging, manipulation, or criticism, even when it's for our own personal development. So why would we imagine they'll accept our nagging, manipulation, and criticism?

Sometimes we won't nurture our loved ones because we're afraid they'll fail and get hurt. We become so fearful for their well-being that we become clingy, controlling and afraid to let them move outside their comfort zones because we may not be able to protect them. We may become so fearful that we limit their growth and make them dependent on us financially or emotionally. We feel they're foolish to trust themselves and that we'll be able to protect them forever when, in truth, we'll never be able to be there indefinitely for them.

Our loved ones can also feel as though we're competing with them. We can fear they'll outgrow us, possibly beyond our understanding. This could be work-related—a skill or a source of knowledge (e.g., family, business). We might feel that, should they become more successful than we are, it will put a spotlight on our own inadequacies and shortcomings. Many people tend to benchmark their sense of worth based on what they're able to contribute to others, such as finances, knowledge or abilities. When it comes to our children, sometimes we can become fearful that their success will mean they won't need us, or want us to remain a part of their lives.

Because of these fears, instead of instilling courage, we can end up infecting others with our fears and insecurities. We want our loved ones to grow; however, we just don't really want them to grow *too much* or *too quickly*, because we may not be able to catch up. Basically, we don't want them to grow faster than us because, to feel appreciated and loved, we feel we'll need to catch up. When we infect others with our own fears, we don't realize we can quash their courage, which can lead them to belittle or suppress ours. Instead of nurturing each other beyond our comfort zones, we can hold each other back.

Relationships are a paradox. The more we push our way so we can be a part of the other person's world, the more s/he can appears to pull away. This is true for many parents and their children. The more we try to remain an essential part of their lives, the less they want us to be. The more we push for our needs to be met, they become less willing to address them. The more we push, the more they push back, fending us off, trying to get away, withdrawing into themselves and not letting us remain an integral part of their emotional world.

Oftentimes, we avoid people who force their way into our lives. But when people let us grow, to appreciate life and ourselves, we often find their presence addictive and intoxicating; we want to spend more time with them. We want them to be a larger part of our lives because the association allows us to see and appreciate the immense value they offer. Frequently, to get what we want we must first give it away selflessly and freely. The more we make sure that others know they matter to us, the more we'll matter to them. This may be why mothers are so fondly looked upon and remembered; their nurturing, love and desire for us to grow make us want to protect our memories of them forever.

It's easy to understand why we should nurture children. While they're on their path to growth, we take time to care for them, allow them to fail, let them struggle, and guide them as they overcome life's challenges without fear of rejection or reprimand. We aren't there to judge, only to pick them up and dust off their hurt, give them a little peck on the cheek, and send them off again. We let them know we're in their lives in meaningful ways.

Whether children or adults, when others let us into their lives to help nurture their growth, it's a gift. And it's a gift to receive that support. We're here to enjoy a journey together, helping each other discover new facets of ourselves. Encouraging them gently with warmth and affection, we help each other realize our potential.

"Grow to become more than your limitations,

and let your loved ones do the same."

Chapter 25

They Hunger for Our Enthusiasm

When a loved one gives, we like to feel their willingness and eagerness to give. We like to see their enthusiasm. When we see they're reluctant to give, or worse, refuse to accommodate our needs, we can begin to feel as if they don't care about us. It can feel as if they're willing to sacrifice our well-being as long as their needs are met. How can we trust a relationship in which we feel our well-being is frequently sacrificed because it isn't convenient for the other person? Their enthusiasm isn't dependent on whether they care for us; it's a question of how much they care.

When fervent effort is made and when initiatives are taken with glee, all doubts are erased. When loved ones put our needs first, we're comforted by the thought that they consider our well-being. And even when they can't meet our needs, we know they still care deeply about us. We love knowing they're trying to meet our immediate needs even as they consider our long-term happiness. This is why effort and enthusiasm are important. The greater effort we show each other, the more we feel cared for.

A lackluster effort on another's part can convey to us that maybe we are pushing too hard or expect too much of them. If this is the case, they may disappear or stop giving all together. This can make us feel like we can't rely on them to meet our needs or give us emotional support. Even though they may not wish to make us feel this way, their unwillingness or lack of enthusiasm can beg the question: *Why should you matter to me?*

It's impossible to feel truly secure and loved when loved ones aren't sure if their partners are reliable. Effort conveys a form of unconditional love; lack of effort conveys conditional love, or the message: *Ask too much of me and I'll stop loving you.*

We worry that if we ask for too much, our partners will stop giving. We feel their love is conditional, that they'll hold back financial assistance, time or affection, for example, if we don't obey or meet certain conditions. To expect our loved ones to tolerate or accept conditional love isn't healthy; it only instills fear and distrust.

Conditional love can also take the form of rejecting or even disowning family members because they want to live their lives differently. Despite not agreeing with loved ones' lifestyle choices, their beliefs, or their career paths (after all, it's their life not ours), rather than belittling them or what they believe will bring them happiness, shouldn't we support them instead? As we mature and grow into the individuals we are right now, we sought the acceptance and understanding of our loved ones. We may even have argued with them and disagreed with their views of the world, but at the end of the day, we still relished their support. Didn't we all struggle with this when we were growing up? Seeking support and understanding is what we continue to struggle with as fully grown adults.

It's all right to expect loved ones to love and treat us in ways we can appreciate. We just need to remember to do the same for them. A good start is to make an effort in areas that are important to our loved ones. We all know how it feels when those we care about show disregard for our feelings and seem to show indifference to our achievements and our pain. We don't want our loved ones to feel the same way about us.

Showing effort doesn't need to be a grand. It's not about being over the top expressive. This was something I struggled with when I was younger. In general, I am not an overly expressive person; showing joy, happiness, and glee does not come naturally. Sometimes displaying these kinds of feelings felt strange and somewhat awkward. But because I wanted to make a difference in my loved ones' lives, over time I've worked on being more expressive, including learning ways to show enthusiasm and encouragement.

I've learned that sometimes it isn't just an issue of enthusiasm - being thrilled and excited for others; it's about *not* being doubtful and disheartened. Sometimes they don't need us to show enthusiasm, just not show disappointment. We've all had an idea, something we want to do, but when we shared it with our loved ones, they shot holes in it. No one wants to constantly spend time with a *"why it won't work"* kind of person, someone who is always pointing all the problems and never offers a solution, advice, encouragement or even a helping hand. These kinds of people have been called "dream stealers." They say they tell us where the problems are because they care, but at the same time, they don't realize how they are killing our dream, and our confidence and enthusiasm for pursuing it.

Rather than telling them why it can't work, the approach can be tweaked, and asking, "*How we can help them succeed?* or *How can we help them overcome their challenge?*" This gives them courage and motivation, and they feel supported. They're more willing to come to us for advice, to share their woes and struggle. They don't feel we are stealing their dream because they feel we are letting them be uniquely who they are.

When it comes to enthusiasm, simple efforts reap tremendous results. A first step: take "resistance" out of our vocabulary — if your partner asks something of you, be willing to accommodate him/her with enthusiasm. In the end, if you don't, they won't for you.

"Don't be a dream stealer;

instead encourage with enthusiasm!"

Words from a Friend

Even though life is full of challenges, it does not mean that this is all that life has to offer. On the flipside of struggle and frustration, there is fulfillment and understanding. Without the former we will not greatly appreciate the other. Learn to accept, or at least tolerate frustration because deep within it we'll find the keys to understanding ourselves.

To be able to journey within ourselves and those we hold dear, to be able to discover what was hidden all this time deep inside all of us is a magical experience. It allows us to unlock the path to our own happiness. But to be able to do so, we must first be willing to embark on the discovery of new ways of living and loving, and let go of the old, worn out paths that seem to only lead to hurt.

It is not an easy path to take, but if we truly seek happiness, we need to let go of our past hurts. We cannot have joy without pain, light without darkness, and success without the possibility of failure. There will be plenty of struggles and plenty of days when everything will feel pointless, or even hopeless. I cannot guarantee these days will not come along; however, what I can promise is if we master the skills within this book, then the days of hurt and frustration will be less frequent, or at least they will not be as daunting. Many of the skills may seem overly simplistic, but they are very powerful when we learn to live by them each and every day, no matter what hardship we may have to endure. People tend to think they need a grand, new or profound idea for them to solve their problems. This is not always true.

No one is born strong; they have just learned to develop their emotional and social skills. Emotional growth and personal development is not only about learning to develop great positive habits, but also about learning to abandon bad ones. In the process of doing this, it is not always easy to look at ourselves, and this will continue to be a challenge no matter what stage of emotional maturity we are at. We all have achieved some decent milestones, but emotional development is not a destination. It is a learning curve, a journey and an ideal towards which we strive.

Congratulations for reading this book, and thank you for taking this journey with me.

If you are reading this, then hopefully your life is now better for it. I hope you challenged some of my views and yourself in the process. There is no point in accepting new conflicting models or concepts if you are unwilling to question their integrity. By understanding where someone is coming from and how they came to their conclusions, we are better equipped to decide if their experiences and insights apply to us.

Lastly, I would like to impart some final words of wisdom. Hopefully, they will act as reminders for you to strive for even more, and continue to let go of your past hurts for your future happiness. These words are etched on my bathroom mirror and are the very same words I have set to live my life by. Let them creep into yours – I hope they will lead you to a better and brighter future.

"Live purposely by going beyond comfort every day. Do not fear the unknown, fear not knowing."

APPENDIX

Love Association Exercise

These are my answers for the Love Association Exercise in Chapter Four. This is what I needed to feel loved, to feel as if I belong in the relationship. Hopefully, it will give you an idea about how to better express yourself. Through completing this exercise with a partner, you can learn to have a much better appreciation of what you and s/he need to feel loved and fulfilled within your relationship.

I feel loved when you...

1. Hug me when I feel down and depressed.

2. Have a smile on your face and happy to see me when I get home tired from work.

3. Tell me you love me.

4. Snuggle up to me on the couch while we watch television.

5. Show your tenderness and express your concerns.

6. Show me your eagerness for sex.

7. Allow me space to be myself and for myself.

8. Allow me to contribute to your life.

9. Encourage me when I seem to have lost my way.

10. Show consideration for me by making efforts for me.

I show my love to you by...

1. Being attentive and caring.

2. Trying to understand your needs.

3. Trying to put your needs before mine.

4. Telling you how much I love you and how much you matter to me.

5. Trying to be a good provider and care taker.

6. Working hard and trying to advance in life to share more of life's luxury with you.

7. Spending time with you.

8. Listening and giving you the attention you deserve.

9. Trying to let go of my own hurt so you can express yours.

10. Thinking of little ways to make things easier for you.

I love you for...

1. Your tenderness and caring nature.
2. Your consideration of others.
3. Your willingness to listen to my needs.
4. Your level-headedness and common sense.
5. Your sensuality.
6. Your upbeat personality.
7. Your kindness to everyone, even strangers.
8. Loving me for who I am, warts and all.
9. Your growth mindset.
10. Your enthusiasm for life.

I love the fact that you...

1. Want the best for me.
2. Always think positively.
3. Have integrity.
4. Have a strong sense of self.
5. Do what's needed, not always what's easy.
6. Don't want to hurt others.
7. Look at my potential and want me to reach it.
8. See the good in me when I don't.
9. Make me want to love you.

10. Want to be a part of my life and want me to be a part of yours.

Acknowledgments

To my older sister, Thi Ly, for teaching me the meaning of courage. Paving your own path to happiness, defiant, and persistent against struggles, you taught me happiness is earned, not just given. You are someone I look up to and admire without end. I love you with all my heart and feel very blessed to have you as a sister.

To Khang (who died so young,) for teaching me friendship. Khang is the first person who made me feel that I belonged – he shared with me the secrets of being a great friend. His death taught me that friends are important, but quality friends are crucial. Thank you and farewell my friend, you live on in memories.

To Tiffany, for the time we spent together. I hope you find love, happiness and everything you desire… even if it isn't with me. I cherish our time spent together for they have left a lasting positive impression for me. You have one of the most beautiful souls.

To Bany, for the many late nights we bounced ideas. Bany, you are monumental, acting as a sounding board and playing the devil's advocate as we refined many of these ideas. You're a walking encyclopedia, with a thirst for knowledge; your clear thinking is just one if many things I admire about you. You are a great friend.

To Alex, for teaching me joy. Alex, you are one of the sweetest people I've ever met. Sincerity is one of your greatest qualities. I admire how you care for people, cherish your friendship, and smile with glee at your enthusiasm for life. You're always ready to welcome others with firm embrace from the very first moment.

To Maree, for allowing me to see the beauty in others' foibles. You are direct, can miss subtleties, and at times say things that might be considered harsh (usually unintentionally), but looking past it all, you are a very sweet girl. You've helped me learn to appreciate people's shortcomings, because they are part of our raw, honest selves. I look forward to your growth and being there for you to lean on if need be, and I know you'll be there for me.

To Trent, for your elegance with words and seductive smile. Trenty, you're a charmer. You can make people fall in love with you just by batting your eyes and giving a cheeky smile. Listening to you wax words and string sentences together, I can't help but gain an appreciation for subtleties. From you, I learned how elegantly used words can leave people gleeful and brimming, and when they are misused and ill-considered they can leave people emotionally battered and bruised.

To Henryk, for your earnest pursuit of happiness that helps remind me that simplicity is beauty. Henryk is tall, of Polish descent and well-bred. He came from a loving home, is muscularly built, good-looking and someone who wants to find love (and yes, I envy you, too). While many people overcomplicate things, they never really notice how simple some of us are, and how much we simply want to love and be loved. Henryk, you're the epitome of this: you want someone to love you, for who you are, taking life one step at a time.

To Sydrah, for your love and affection, and tolerating my not-so-great qualities. Relationships aren't easy and will never be — emotions are forever present. You remind me that we all show love in our own ways, and at times we struggle to show it in ways that others can appreciate.

To Heather, Sandy, Angela, Kristin, Laura, Marley, and Hillery — my editors — for your elegance with the English language. Some have it, some don't. While I may not, they seem to be brimming with it. I want to thank you for giving the book the much-needed style that was so desperately missing. They went well above and beyond what was ever expected. The book would not be in existence right now if it were not for them.

Seeking More Answers

Each of these books offers their own wealth of knowledge and understanding. By creating better tools and understanding, we can gain more of the things we want in life. These books are a great start for anyone:

48 Laws of Power: Robert Greene

Awaken the Giant Within: Anthony Robbins

Blink: Malcolm Caldwell

Definitive Guide to Body Language: Allan Pease

Destructive Emotions: Daniel Goleman

Developing the Leader Within You: John C. Maxwell

Emotional Intelligence: Daniel Goleman

Emotions Revealed: Paul Eckman

How to Argue and Win Every Time: Jerry Spence

How to Win Friends and Influence People: Dale Carnegie

Influence: Robert Ciadini

Getting To Yes: William Ury & Roger Fisher

Maximum Achievement: Brian Tracey

Men Are From Mars, Women Are From Venus: John Gray

Nonviolent Communication: Marshall Rosenberg

Neuro-Linguistic Programming: John Grinder, Richard Bach & Robert Dilts

Over The Top: Zig Ziglar

Outliers: Malcolm Caldwell

Psycho-Cybernetics: Maxwell Maltz

Speaking Peace: Marshall Rosenberg

Sperm Wars: Robin Baker

Social Intelligence: Daniel Goleman

The Art of Seduction: Robert Greene

The Brain That Changes Itself: Norman Doidge

The Chase: Samantha Brett

The Five Love Languages: Gary Chapman

The Leader Within You: Dale Carnegie

The Lies We Believe: Chris Thurman

The Magic of Thinking Big: David J. Schwartz

The One Minute Manager: Kenneth Blanchard

The Selfish Gene: Richard Dawkins

The Seven Habits of Highly Effective People:

Stephen R. Covey

The Seven Principles for Making a Marriage Work: John M. Gottman

The Six Pillars of Self-Esteem: Nathanael Brandon

Think and Grow Rich: Napoleon Hill

Tipping Point: Malcolm Caldwell

Unlimited Power: Anthony Robbins

Why Men Don't Listen and Women Can't Read Maps: Barbara Pease & Allan Pease

www.ingramcontent.com/pod-product-compliance
Lightning Source LLC
LaVergne TN
LVHW051551070426
835507LV00021B/2518